THE

Includes the diary
One Hundred Days of a Father's Mourning

To Marica.

Lots of love & light

always

Alan x

Written, Illustrated and Published
by Alan Stuttle
NDD, RCA. London

Typeset, Printed and Bound by
The McRay Press, Scarborough, North Yorkshire YO12 4AS, UK

Alan Stuttle NDD RCA London
Artist, Author & Publisher

The Alan Stuttle Gallery, 34 North Marine Road, Scarborough,
North Yorkshire YO12 7PE, England
Tel: +44 (0)1723 354080   email: alanstuttle@aol.com

1st Edition April 2007

Typeset, designed, printed and bound by
The McRay Press of Scarborough, North Yorkshire YO12 4AS

ISBN 978-0-9555636-0-7

Front cover illustration is a Water colour painted by Alan Stuttle
of The Tree planted in Bundaberg, Australia
in memory of Caroline...

THE BRIDGE

Includes the diary
One Hundred Days of a Father's Mourning

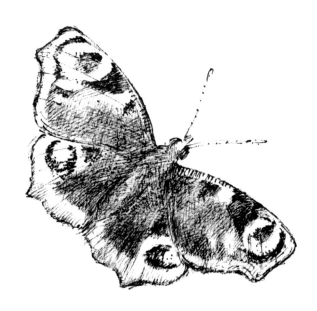

by Alan Stuttle
NDD, RCA. London

Forward

It was a news story which shocked a nation and beyond, involving a beautiful young woman with her whole life in front of her.

As a journalist of more than 30 years I have had to cover many tragedies which have affected me deeply, but as the mother of a teenage daughter, none more so than events in a quiet backwater in Australia which led to a terrible murder at the hands of an opportunist thief. Backpacking her way round one of the most visited countries in the world, Caroline Stuttle was having a wonderful time, experiencing different places and meeting new friends. Her excitement shone through in the texts and phonecalls sent halfway round the world to her family and friends. Then she was murdered. And there the story might end but it won't. Caroline Stuttle's death will not be in vain. With great strength and fortitude her parents were determined her short life will remain a testament to all that is good in the world... a reminder that young people should be encouraged to fly the nest and grow as individuals and, God willing, return home safe and sound with their horizons broadened.

A charity offering advice to young travellers has been set up in her name...and then there is this book, a father's thoughts on the death of his most precious daughter. I read Alan Stuttle's diary as he was actually writing it when I travelled with him and Caroline's brother to Australia for the first time to visit the spot where she died. It is true it makes painful reading. But through the despair and disbelief there is a message of love and hope for us all, that life, no matter how short, is precious and for living.

I am proud to have been asked to write this forward and to have met this young woman's family. They are very special and, therefore, so was she.

Christa Ackroyd
January 2007

The days before

The days before the murder of my Daughter Caroline were strange, the feelings I had were of great emotion and inner turmoil not knowing why. I had been on the south cliff side of Scarborough painting a clock tower, not knowing that it was to become a very well known view as part of a new TV. series.

That day I, for some reason, was thinking of my children of when they were young and in some way wishing to turn the clock back.

Looking at the past and thinking of the future, dreams and hopes I have, not ever expecting something so devastating was about to happen, that was to change my circumstances so very extensively. It was to be the worst nightmare anyone could have, an impossible scenario in all ways imaginable. It was to be the hardest time of my life.

This experience has enabled me to recognise my real friends and to appreciate them, I received letters, texts and e-mails world wide, also traveled to the other side of our world.

I have received letters from friends from the early part of my life, school friends from when I was five years old in Cheshire to now, when I am 65 years old living North Yorkshire.

Caroline meant the world to me and still does, yet within this awful tragedy she has introduced me to parts of our world I would never have thought of visiting.

Not only have I experienced new places but my son Richard, Caroline's brother, has now travelled Australia extensively seeing (the same and) more of the spectacular landscapes and sunsets that Caroline once saw.

I dedicate this book to my daughter Caroline's memory with grateful thanks for her life, and to all the experiences and love shown to me as I journey through this life until one day, if it is to be so, we will be reunited in that other world yet to be explored.

Chapter One

The world has become a smaller place in so many ways. Caroline has touched so many hearts and minds throughout the countries that it is impossible to put love into words.

How can I write something that was never meant to be written, the spirit of universal unity in this great sadness, but in a strange way great joy and hope for future years?

In the hundred days of writing this diary I have felt the deepest despair, I have been aware of universal love and prayer, shed tears I never thought would end, felt so much pain in my heart I thought it would break.

I have met friends that I have not seen for many years, felt anger about the futile things that people say and do to each other, felt also the pain and disappointment about the thoughtless remarks people say.

I have travelled to Australia where my daughter was so happy during the last few days of her short life; shed tears with my son Richard at the spot where she died. I have done what I had to do to say goodbye to someone so irreplaceable in my life.

As an artist I have painted pictures in a healing way, to be creative in these awful circumstances is very important as a healing process. We must go on with our lives, time and life still have to be lived through, and it does not stop with the murder of Caroline.

I have tried to put over, in the press and on the television, that we must not let these awful tragedies put us or our children off travelling to discover different countries and cultures. To discover something about ourselves. It is important to meet people with different ideas and religions, perhaps it will bring about an understanding that we are all children of the same God (if you wish to call it that). We should live in harmony, not murder, war and devastation that we have in many ways throughout our world.

Australia gave me the opportunity to paint Sydney harbour bridge. It would have been one of Caroline's most exciting times at the earlier part of her tour, before going to Brisbane and then on to Bundaberg to a very different bridge.

Sydney harbour bridge to me is like a bridge of angels as it tells of the crossing of the vast river of life and onwards into heaven where we will all be met by our guardian angels and loved ones known in this world.

4

One should never be afraid of death, it is likened to going across a bridge to another world that is free from pain, where we may see people or the spirit of a person for what he or she is, not for the material possessions they have collected along the way of life.

It is for what we do in life that we are remembered for. The colours we wear in our hearts we take with us on our long journey into eternity. The one thing I know for sure is that we go forward on a tide of love because love conquers all.

Chapter two

Earlier this year I visited the Yorkshire Dales where Caroline and I visited many times. Whilst finishing a painting I had started sometime previously when we had been visiting Hawes, a rainbow appeared in the sky, so consequently I put it in the painting.

On the return journey I saw three prisms of rainbow in the sky, something I had never before experienced. I wondered if this was a sign of something to come.

On another Dales visit, after the winter snows, I retraced the steps Caroline and I had walked in previous years, to the caravan site near Hawes where we had seen stars so clearly, moving lights in the night sky, this has always been a very happy memory.

Over the last year I have been travelling to all these places I shared with my children and remembering the joy's of their childhood.

Filey was a special place because of it's safe beaches and unspoilt surroundings, Scarborough, which is my current home, with the castle, the parks, the beach with it's rock pools, the wind to carry the children's kites. I have painted this scene many times along with the bucket and spade times and running in the sea.

North Yorkshire moors with the beautiful churches where private prayers are said. Hutton Le Hole where streams were paddled, have all been visited in very recent months, especially the church at Lastingham. These are all places I have painted and loved very much and are thankful to have been able to introduce to my children. For them to enjoy the beauty of nature, feeling the wind in their hair and the sun on their faces. These memories are with me for ever.

Who was to know what was to occur next?

On the week prior to Caroline's trip to Australia, as a Dad is expected to do, I met up with her to buy her the last minute things she needed (rucksack etc.) I am still paying for these, thank goodness for my flexible friend. Caroline always enjoyed it when the sales assistant said "Oh! It is Alan Stuttle, the artist"; we would always have a chuckle.

Previous to this I wrote her a bon voyage card on which I wrote "Caroline, you will have the time of your life, go for your dreams, some will come true. One of my dreams was to have a little girl like you and my dream came true. I love you very much DAD XXXX".

During the trip I thought she might get short of money although she had worked hard and saved plenty, she knew I would top her up towards the end of the trip.

The days before the murder of my daughter I should have been in Italy but felt tired and listless and wanted to be on my own in my studio in Scarborough, I was thinking of my children when they were small and needed me as I now needed them.

I just wanted to paint landscapes and flowers of my beautiful Yorkshire for the rest of my life, but I knew in my heart some change was coming.

That first week in April the weather was so beautiful I could go out and paint. Only days later my life, as I knew it, was to change so very much, will the sunshine be gone forever?

On the evening of Caroline's murder after having a more restful day, still feeling weary, went to bed early. After about four hours I awoke with a strange feeling and a fluttering like palpitation around my heart, my thoughts were am I having a heart attack but there were no other symptoms. It was a very gentle feeling, I then must have gone back to sleep to be awoken by the sound of someone coming into my bedroom. It was the police. My life sentence had begun.

The Diary

When I decided to write down my thoughts and feelings, I looked around for an almost empty diary or book and to my hand came the diary that Caroline had bought me inside the cover says "To Dad, Happy Christmas, lets hope it's a good 1999. Lots of love, Caroline".

Day 1
11th April 2002

At around five o'clock I was woken up by footsteps up the stairs of my flat. Into my bedroom came two male police officers, and they informed me that my little girl had been murdered in Bundaberg Australia.

I went hysterical and don't remember much that day.

Someone has killed my baby.

The feeling of none reality, a dream or nightmare it can't be true.

Chris and Jane, two of my staff, came with the police. As key holders they were marvellous, they took me out for a walk by the church where Caroline and I had walked a few weeks before. The sun was shining but I felt so cold in my heart.

The police stayed until we got back and then a close friend, Brian, arrived and once the police could see I was being cared for they left.

I rang Janet in Birmingham and screamed "They have killed my baby", hysterical once again. The police asked Janet to come as soon as possible, which she did.

I picked up on the shear pain and terror of my daughter's death; I will not describe what I felt.

The police were wonderful, it must have been so hard for them to have to break news like this. Later that day I was assigned a personal police liaison officer who remained with me, not allowing me to do anything, protecting me from media etc.

Day 2
12th April

Don't remember much of this day, Foreign and Commonwealth office rang, Megan Hunt, British Consulate, Queensland police deputy commissioner all rang to try and help, all rather vague, could not take it in. Brian came again. Janet looked after me all day. I'm in a daze, could not write.

Day 3
13th April

Could not sleep much again, a living nightmare spent the day looking at all the paintings of Caroline I had painted, I wanted them all around.

Caroline's mother, Marjorie and Richard, Caroline's brother, were also being looked after by friends and the police in York.

Many telephone calls from Australia and the police again, were told the report was on Television and in the press, could not bear to look. Our liaison officer, Sarah, came and stayed all day giving help and advice, what a strength. I would not have known where to start. Brian called in again with more support.

Prior to this happening, Janet and I had been invited to dinner at our friends, Chris and Dawn's house, Dawn contacted us on hearing the news, I decided we should go it was a great help to bring a little normality and sanity for us both, our friends were very compassionate yet we could allow some lightness of heart at times, even laughter. Talking of Caroline made me feel proud. Under the circumstances, a very pleasant evening and the wonderful meal helped, although I don't think I tasted much.

It is important to carry on or is it?

Day 4
14th April

Not much sleep again, am I still in a dream?

Margaret, a friend from Doncaster, came to spend a couple of days to help and support both Janet, and myself. Margaret gave us a treatment of reflexology (foot massage), which relaxed us.

More telephone calls from Australia, Sarah, my liaison officer, again giving advice and updated information.

Brian came again; he lets me get it off my chest.

Day 5
15th April

Another day dawned bright, slept a little better, perhaps the reflexology helped.

Had so many people ring with prayers and love you could feel it. Many cards and letters, overwhelming.

Phone calls again from Australia; Sarah came and reported on updated police information.

I am going out today to Filey with Janet and Margaret to paint, for Caroline, a little water colour of where she used to play on the beach. Weather was beautiful. Margaret and Janet are so good.

It was good to do just something, makes you feel better to remember past times and to say goodbye. This painting is to go into the coffin with Caroline.

Brian was also in touch that day.

Day 6
16th April

Awoken at 6.30am by telephone call from British Consulate to inform of church service being held in Bundaberg for Caroline and for me to offer a few words. Can't really remember saying words, just let my heart speak. Sarah came with updates.

Went to Hutton Le Hole and painted for Caroline. I went to the river, it was beautiful.

Up on the moors where Caroline would have found a stream to paddle in. Sat on a rock to paint and the sun came out for that short while.

Had lunch at the Forge café and then on to Lastingham Church, said a prayer.

Felt drained, I am out of it.

Unable to read all the letters and cards today. Dreading tomorrow.

Lastingham Church, nr Hutton-le-Hole

Day 7

17th April

The next worse day of my life. Funeral times, hymns and choosing a coffin was the most distressing thing you can ever do for your 19 year old daughter, with all the world at her finger tips my heart was breaking but kept things going at the house. Richard was devastated, and Caroline's boyfriend is so very distraught.

The police are wonderful, Margaret and Jan wonderful, collected wild flowers and made a sketch of Scarborough.

Caroline start's her journey back to England tomorrow. Feel sick.

Day 8

18th April

Richard and Ian are going to meet Caroline at Manchester along with the police, they will follow the car back to York District hospital, they felt it was something that they should do, I could not.

Felt numb today. Could not write much. Cards and messages coming more and more, Caroline has touched many hearts in her short life.

Usual visit from Sarah and call from Brian. How will I get through tomorrow!

Day 9

19th April

Police take me to the mortuary of York hospital. Saw the little body of Caroline, my daughter, I cannot describe the feeling of devastation I felt on seeing the broken skin on her face and her little body wrapped in a white linen sheet. I steadied myself and entered the room where she lay so quiet now, at peace. I touched her hand that was laid above the sheet it was cold and stiff with the feeling of wax. I kissed her bruised head and hair. Last time Caroline was in hospital was when she was born. Now I was saying goodbye in the mortuary. Part of me died that day, yet the prayers of my friends kept me strong.

Who could do this to such a young innocent and very beautiful young girl, what kind of creature was it so despicable I can hardly speak or write of it.

A few short days ago I had an e-mail from Caroline saying how she was enjoying herself and my heart sang with joy, now in a few short days she will be laid to rest near her home in Huntington, York.

Given into the cold bosom of the gentle ground, my precious little girl, gone from sight, but never in spirit.

Oh, God, the days are so long and my heart bleeds along with so many. Am I in a dream? I need to wake up.

Day 10
20th April

Date fixed for funeral Tuesday 23rd April.

Feel awful, did yesterday really happen. Can I go on?

Don't feel like writing today, feel sick and angry, the pain continues, why me? But why not.

More telephone calls, so very- very tired. Had flowers from police and a Benevolent Society.

Day 11
21st April

Feel terrible today. Painting a picture in oils of the flowers the police sent to me, they are beautiful.

Have to get out, Janet takes me to Filey again, have lunch and walk around.

Many telephone calls, Brian, as always, he is so good. (Brian is a student from Essex).

I rang Richard, we will collect him tomorrow to see Caroline for the last time, it's awful, things could not be worse. Also the one-upmanship should be stopped ASAP.

Let's have some respect for Caroline.

Write press hand out.

Weather beautiful.

Day 12
22nd April

Went to see Caroline for the last time – in this world. She looked so small, bruised and felt cold and very different. The worst sight in the world for any father of a 19-year-old daughter, but she is eternally beautiful.

I placed my gift for eternity with her by her right hand, and placed a little crucifix from Assisi. All now is finished.

Richard and Ian came to say goodbye, they were so very brave, I was proud of them.

I gave Richard and Caroline the same gift (of different materials) on the last day that I could. The chapter ends.

Richard needs to be quiet, he can come to Scarborough.

The news of a charity was announced, I feel it is too soon. I am too upset to bother.

I need to lay my child to rest first.

It was good to see Grant and Jean from Canada, Auntie Mildred and Terri. It is nice to be family.

Grant brought me a dream catcher from America and a wonderful sweatshirt. Even now I am given so much love and care.

It's just not real; I must soon wake up into a world that I know.

I must keep doing painting etc. Caz would have wanted that.

The house at Huntington was like a circus, so many people milling around like busy little ants. It is a time of sorrow not party time. Not in good taste, just say you are sorry and go away. We need space, letting personal problems go away, at least for the time being. There have even been so called mediums giving messages from Caroline. I feel sick, it is disgusting.

Tomorrow I have to face another day. God help me get through this terrible ordeal.

Day 13
23rd April

This is the worst day anyone could have; I have to say goodbye to a beautiful daughter of 19 murdered by God knows what (not human) for a telephone.

I shall have to do my best to keep it dignified and with gentle love, most of all for Richard and Marjorie, the last time we will be unified in this world.

It is going to be hell and heaven at the same time.

Last night a fire started opposite my gallery in Scarborough, what else can happen today?

I have had so much love from friends and people I have met from all over the world, this has been wonderful. The unity of love, which binds us all, is wonderful.

Day 14
24th April

Yet another day, beautiful weather, spring is here. I needed space after yesterday, so have been painting watercolours of Scarborough South Bay, it is good to be outside and mix with people. Life goes on though the pain will not stop.

The press have been very good with coverage, but I don't like reading it, sometime I must.

Cried in the evening, Janet is so good, what would I do without her love and care, I am a lucky man.

I keep thinking of Caroline's little body now in a grave, only a few days ago she was full of life and love, now lies black and broken, in the darkness of a grave. I need the light - so much I have missed out on in life, most has been taken from me, now, most of all, my beloved daughter.

Day15
25th April

Yet another day. Weather bright, made the effort to get out and paint watercolours. Feel empty. Lots more cards.

Went to dinner with Brian and Mary. It felt good to get out and eat with good friends. Slept better that night.

Day 16
26th April

Went and painted in my studio, still feel empty. It will never be the same. I would like Janet to stay with me, she is a wonderful lady and knows what I have been doing.

Cancelled going to work at the college at Stansted, don't think I could go on with it.

Grant has been taken ill in York hospital, suspected gall problem.

Painted at Robin Hoods Bay.

Day 17
27th April   (17 days dead)

Went to York. Got things from Caroline's car, little toy, tapes, a pen and a purple cushion. Not much, even the little red car looked sad yet started up first time.

Went to the grave, the rainbow wreath still looks fresh and many more flowers. Richard has written a wonderful card, what you did not achieve in life may you achieve in death.

I did not feel anything in that cemetery, only emptiness, thinking of my child being cold and dead beneath the earth. She cannot feel the warm sun or smell the spring air or hear the birds sing.

Went to the gallery, it was empty too. Did not stay long.

Phoned about Grant, he is ok. Thank God.

Feel very empty, sad and angry at our loss. Part of me has died with Caz. I do so hurt.

Cried in the evening again. Janet is so good to me.

I wish I could wake up now and all will be back to as it was.

Day 18
28th April

Yet another day, more news on the TV. about Caroline on and on.

It seems an eternity and nightmare at the same time, this cannot be right.

I tried painting but it didn't work out very well today, it rained and was cold and windy.

Why should my daughter have been killed for a mobile phone and a few pounds she had worked hard for? I simply can't think anymore.

I begin my life sentence, this month part of me died.

Sarah, the police officer, came again today but no news.

Janet is so caring I think I shall stay in her care for many years if she will have me. She knows me and all that has gone before, no lies no nonsense. Trying to get a few drawings sorted and signing prints, need to do

something.
The hurt is unbearable.

Day 19
29th April
Another day. Went to John's at the farm to get my V.W. caravanette sorted out, something different to do. New starter motor needed.
Wind and rain.
The pain and loss keeps on. It would be nice to go to the Dales again in the V.W. and remember Caroline and our little jaunts, one with her dog.
Just empty and lost, never to see my daughter again.
Very tired after a day at John's, lots of work.
Very down.

Day 20
30th April
Went to York early in the morning, Then to the gallery, felt very old.
A stranger said how very sorry she was.
Alan says I could put my paintings in his gallery, that's nice. I have lost my spring or spirit, indeed I have. Saw Michael, must get sorted ASAP.
Caroline's heart stopped twenty days ago along with mine. May retire now. No reason to go on.

Day 21
1st May
Caroline is Dead. My little girl. I simply can't take it in. All the go and interest in my work has faded, yet the trees and blossoms are beautiful, the weather dramatic.
Went to Durham to take a painting. Nice day out with Janet. She has been very kind.
The shops, of course are in trouble (Sale? – Closing down? – Retirement?)
Police commissioner in Australia rang with an update.
Some silly person rang this evening and tried to give me a psychic message supposed to be from Caroline, I could not cope. They should not do it, it is in very bad taste, not kind at all when someone has lost someone so precious. I believe it is for their own ego.

Day 22
2nd May
Weather fine. Painted in the morning. Brian and Mary came for coffee with us.
Went to paint a few churches, went quite well but rained all afternoon.
Problems at galleries again, all is a potential minefield.
Divorce settlement, failing business and the death of my Daughter. At 63 is all that I need. I think I have been totally destroyed in all ways, nothing

else to lose.

Phoned Richard, he has been left on his own too long. Must give him some money.

I feel empty. Looked at the old texts from Caroline, only a few weeks ago, time goes so slow.

I must have been given the strength of Angels.

Day 23
3rd May

Went to York, gallery for sale. Did a little press notice to thank my staff and the people of York for their love, kindness and support. People came in to see me, it has rained on and off all day so could not get outside, I am retiring from York, I've had enough, have seen the total of the over draught, It is just not worth it.

Went to see John at the farm, had a little tinker with my VW. Just to keep working on anything helps the time go.

I have been to hell.

Lot's of letters and cards still coming, all people want to say is sorry.

I was due to be at Stansted Hall this week. No way I can face it!

Day 24
4th May

Press coverage of me closing the gallery, thanking staff and loyal friends for the past 30 years.

Yet another day working in the gallery in York. Painted outside, felt a little more light hearted today and the weather is beautiful. Still get tired very quickly.

Still can't believe it, should have been at the college but it would not have been a good idea. Problems if you do and problems if you don't. Can't win. Must get things sorted ASAP.

Day 25
5th May

An awful day. Don't know where I am or what to do. The weather is bright but cold and windy. Made an attempt to paint outside but too windy.

Had to rest this afternoon, did not sleep well last night, thoughts of loss, death and cheating people are mostly on my mind. Keep thinking of Caroline in a little grave, cold and dark with peoples gifts and mine locked away forever in a casket of wood. No sunlight will fall on her blackened and bruised little body. I am truly in hell. No one should have all this at once put upon them.

Patience has given way to anger and rage at what has been done to my family and darling Daughter. Vengeance is mine, sayeth the Lord and surely it must be so.

The days are long, nearly four weeks since my last text message from Caroline.

Day 26
6th May

Four weeks since Caroline was murdered and since my last text.

Another day full of problems, even at the gallery with a stupid domestic, no, gentleman, had to dial 999 as if I haven't had enough.

Friends rang from Stansted Hall with best wishes and many prayers.

Bob rang from Canada, had a long chat, it felt better, but still feel empty and angry with one thing and another.

Yet another problem to sort out, get rid of gallery etc. ASAP. need a complete change of area. Weather dull and wet. Worked in York.

Press in Scarborough may do some good.

God, it's going to be a long life time but must keep going. Think – would Caroline want this???

Keep going, keep praying.

Day 27
7th May

Another day, not very good but managed to get through.

TV. rang. May do a little piece about events later. Did a little radio talk, all ok. Mentioned keeping the diary which may become a book to help other grieving parents. Mail on Sunday rang, may do an article with them. Janet took me to Birmingham for a break. So many problems with the galleries it's not real. I feel so very let down in all ways. This, along with the death of Caroline, hurts so very much.

17

Lots of phone calls and letters from strangers as well as friends.

It's not the grief, it's so many other things that are going on, perhaps it's a healing in itself to be so distracted with everyday drama and business etc. Some people have no conceivable feelings of what is going on inside, and one can only put on a brave face and hope that future times will be more relaxed.

Richard is in London, it is good for him to get away with his friend, away from the circus that is going on at the house.

To lose a Daughter, for a Father, is the end of the world, but while there is light we must go on getting all thoughts of gloom out of our mind, using energy to think positively of our young people in future years.

My friend from Scarborough rang, she is a reformed alcoholic, one drink and she will die. Me - I must be positive – depression and my heart and spirit will die.

Almost one month now. Sweet Jesus, pray for the mourning parents of children.

Day 28
8th May

Went away with Jan, there was a great need to get away for a rest and a change of company, it has been horrific in all ways.

Mail rang regarding interview about Caroline. I feel stronger so will do it. (A Father's view of a murdered Daughter).

Radio York telephone interview. BBC. Look North TV. went well. Some rest.

Have done a little painting that helps, and felt better doing something to get the feelings out.

Enjoy life, the sun, the times, do your best while there is still light. Be brave, go with your dreams and hopes. No news about the killer of my daughter, I am sure things are going alone at the right pace.

Day 29

9th May

Yet another day, feel tired and empty.

Grant and Jean have invited Jan and I to Canada, sorry not to have seen much of them this time, as they say, I am always with them with my paintings, that means a lot at this point in time.

Not much of a rest day, going to give an interview to the Mail on Sunday, it may be of some use to someone.

A friend rang, just back from Canada, devastated at the news but informed me that already my words have had an affect as her friends granddaughter has gone backpacking to Australia and the message has gone home about staying in two's and keeping in contact. So that gives me hope.

Strange coincidences come out at times like this. The journalist for the mail mentioned she had been looking at a picture of mine as where she was staying happened to be a mutual friend. Small world.

Interview went well I hope.

Not much rest these days, head muzzy, yet it does help to talk about how things are going.

Very great response to BBC. Interview regarding my tribute to Caroline.

Christa rang regarding the interview, seems to have gone well, lots of interest.

Day 30

10th May

A month on. Young people have the power themselves to stop these grey people from stealing mobile phones from young girls and fish and chips from an elderly lady.

My Daughter was murdered for her mobile phone by the very type of person she was in the future going to try and help. Caroline had a place at Manchester University to study criminal psychology.

The streets need to be rid of this virus so our young and old people can live in freedom, not allowing the thief to rule.

Stay strong and nothing will have the power to destroy your lives with fear, we must not lose any more of our talented young people in this way.

Remember the Beckhams of this world, follow their example, have a strong will to win and a power in their bodies to go for a result.

Did telephone interview for radio York, just spoke from the heart.

More TV. interest.

Not a good day, felt very tired.

Day 31

11th May

Another day, felt very tired, stayed in bed till about 9.30am slept well.

Just painted in Scarborough, dull in the morning beautiful in the afternoon. Painted but could not concentrate very well though.

Richard coming next week and that should be good. I need to spend some time with him.

Very tired indeed have no energy, but carrying on. Think positive not negative. People are sending prayers.

Couple fighting in the street, man after girl. What do you do, get involved, leave alone, call police, girl looked scared but then her friends came to split them up, obviously a lovers tiff but very unsettling.

Will ring or text Richard.

Day 32
12th May

The sun is shining but anger in my heart against the stupidity in this world. People can be so cruel to each other.

The weather is beautiful, will go out and paint.

Paul rang with words of comfort. We must go and see Mary and Paul soon.

Wonderful write up by Christa about Caroline, saying about my diary.

Going down again, not a good day it turns out, getting very depressed and have had panic attacks, feeling the emptiness.

Caroline is all around me, a little girl dressed in pink. Oh how my heart hurts, aches and bleeds. I pray this pain goes away.

A friend text 'you are a real gentleman' whatever that may mean.

Condolences from people in the street, people look at me in a different way, you can feel it, very quiet, just a pat on the shoulder or a handshake or the words 'I am really sorry'.

Caroline was a Daddy's girl, pity the time has sped away in this world.

Auntie Mildred said I must keep on and not let things get to me, but it is so hard and hurts so much. Nothing else has any meaning except life, which can be so quickly put out at any time of your life, at the beginning or at the end.

Will text or ring Richard.

Tears very often today.

Day 33
13th May

Did not sleep very well, many problems on my mind, along with the death of our Daughter. Marjorie and Richard must be feeling so much pain too. Perhaps it is selfish of me to think of myself, but I am feeling so very empty and angry over silly things and people that mean nothing in the broader view of things.

Time heals, so I know, but how and in what way?

I found the painting I did for Caroline on the day she was born along with the words, and the painting I was doing on the day she was murdered. Did a little tribute to Caroline with Look North with Peter and team. Did very well with one thing and another.

Very tired and still angry with the nonsense. Caroline is dead that should be the main thing. It is important to keep going, it's not important what I write or paint, be positive, don't get negative. Use the power from the positive, encouraging our young people to go forward into their future.

I have a life sentence so does my family. I know I shall never see my Daughter again, I don't want anyone to go here, it's hell. (I must go on and do it for Caroline) This is the most important thing.

Feeling so tired, must put my feet up and rest, as difficult as it is when you have been used to a busy life. I have to remember that my body can only take so much, so I listen to it, especially at 63.

Life changes, that's all, we become wiser, only after the experience.

I am pleased that I went for my dream at 58 years old, It had to move me on.

Working on radio with Jenny Murray on Woman's hour Thursday.

There may be a possibility of going to Bundaberg.

Day 34
14th May

Richard came over last night, it was nice to see him. I am very proud of how he is coping with all this turmoil and upset in his life.

He very much needs space and time on his own, it was good to see him skateboarding this morning in the fresh air of Scarborough, perhaps too fresh.

Richard has gone for a long walk on the beach, it will do him good, clear his mind perhaps.

Tried to do a little painting of Venice, felt tired and could not concentrate for long (go by remote).

Press from Australia rang to see if I would go to Australia and when, and did I blame the people of Bundaberg. Of course not.

Daily Mail rang, they would like to publish some of my rantings, it would be nice but I am no writer, only a Dad.

Had a cry, not for too long though. God, I feel empty inside. The loss sometimes is unbearable, Time moves so slow, I wish I could get back to painting.

Richard says I was not a bad Dad, praise indeed!

Caroline and Richard had been close over the years, I know he has many things he wants to say, but that is for him not me.

Marjorie and I are pleased to have had two wonderful children who are independent of mind and spirit. Nothing else matters in the broader view of life, even though one of our children is dead in body, she will always live on in our hearts. Perhaps this is the true meaning of immortality, so long as they are remembered.

Day 35
15th May

Felt a little more positive this morning. Lots of practical things to do. The anger and problems of galleries and personal to be put on one side.

Janet went to the doctors for a note for her work, I don't think I can manage on my own at this moment in time, what a wonderful lady she is, taking care of all the practical things that have to be done. I too have a note from my doctor, being self-employed I don't expect any practical help, I don't expect anything from anywhere, never had. My work has always been my reward, and the strength and encouragement from family and friends.

Feel rather tired now.

A very nice lady came to interview me and perhaps it will do some good. Richard, Jan & I had a lovely walk to Peasholm Park. It is a beautiful place and it was a walk back in time.

Need to get back to some painting.

Very tired today, I wonder what it is all about.

Richard may write about how he feels and I may be able to include it with these thoughts of mine of the death of Caroline in a book.

Phoned a company regarding my business.

Day 36
16th May

Beautiful day. Had a good sleep, feel quite rested. I have found it most important to rest and sleep.

Try to put all the thoughts in your mind out of the way and replace them with thoughts of future sunny days and the happy times of the past away from all this turmoil as this only keeps you awake. We can not change things, we have to go on for the sake of our loved ones and perhaps for future times and people.

Went to Manchester, what a journey, no more trains for me.

Did the interview with Jenny Murray, went ok. but the subject does not get any easier. Six hours on a train is not good for a fifteen minute interview. It got me out, it was different and life goes on.

Perhaps it is good to get out into the rush of life again, it takes your mind off your problems and gives you trains and the chaos of people rushing about, as life does go on in the outside world. Good to be back home with Jan's healing TLC.

Day37
17th May

Beautiful morning. Paying a few bills, need to get my house in order, sorting papers putting them in order, Jan's good at that.

Today I paid for Caroline's Funeral, that's one more thing out of the way. Not very pleasant.

Feel a little more positive today, yet the cold inside never seems to go away.

I just need to relax, I think I have done enough up to now, just need to ring Australia regarding Richard & me.

Keep positive and your mind open to new ideas. Need to get an exhibition of my paintings, clear them out and maybe sell some. I need a new start, a change of life.

That which was warm is now so cold
That which is lost can not grow old
That love you gave me will always be
Your heart and love with me will ever be.
Dad..xx

Worked a little outside in Scarborough, nice change, met people again, weather good in the morning but cold afternoon. Had lunch at the Clock Café, very nice.

Walking back to the gallery met an old friend I met 30 years ago in York, more sad news, a mutual friend, Alan has died the same time as Caroline. So much bad news. Into every life a little rain must fall, but this is over the top!

Felt tired but started a new painting of Bath Abbey for Christmas cards.

Press want more photographs tonight, this should be the end of it, I need to get back to paint and relax.

Day 38
18th May

A bad night, car alarm going off from 10.30pm – 7.30am, left feeling very restless.

Was going to York but weather so bad decided to stay and paint in the studio. Just finishing off things, nothing major.

It felt quite nice to paint in the studio though felt tired after about an hour or so.

Sarah, our Police liaison officer, came to see us, no news from Australia, but we passed to her a strange letter we had received from Australia.

Slept a lot on and off during the day. People came in to give their sympathy's it is nice to have everyone's support.

Just feel tired and worn out today, perhaps it's the weather.

Richard texted, he will come over this week, Margaret is back from her holidays and Janette from Essex texted me a hug. It means a lot, makes me feel better in myself, but can't stop thinking of Caroline lying so dead and cold under the earth in such eternal darkness.

No telephone calls today, just general finishing off and getting sorted.

My poor darling Daughter, so much promise destroyed in such an awful way.

I don't cry so much. I just hurt inside.

Day 39
19th May

Going to York, find it important to keep in touch with the business, but only when I feel I am ready. People and life still goes on and people have been so very good to us all, most respectful in all ways.

Phone call from Italy with much love, more news from the south that another fellow artist is not well, I shall have to direct some prayers to them.

Feel a little better but the pain won't go away.

Krista rang with thoughts on the Australia visit, it needs to be used in a positive way: helping to encourage our youngsters, from them will come our children of the future.

If we all stopped doing what our hearts tell us, the world would be a desolate place, full of grey inadequate people who take drugs for their hopes, which only fade and chase money which is of little worth in the universe of things.

Love is the only thing that unites us all. Even if my Daughter is now dead (murdered) to this world she will live on in my heart always and she will inspire me to work on my hopes and dreams to be a better person and at the age of 63 years to enjoy more fully what I have left to do. Yes I will mourn and weep always for her and for the children she may have had, my would be grandchildren. With Caroline's hopes and dreams I hope to carry them forward by giving confidence to our young people. To go for their dreams and ambitions allowing their hearts and minds to be touched by the enthusiasm for life that Caroline had, her life then will most certainly have been worth while and not in vain. Though Caroline's life was short I have many memories, as a child she said to me one day whilst walking in a field covered with snow "Daddy I could walk with you forever " and it shall be so, for I know one thing, the love we hold for our family and friends can never die (I shall once again take her small hand in mine).

Day 40
20th May

Bad night, lots of dreams, last one about Caroline & wonderful blue flowers I awoke in tears. I feel like I am having two lives now joy and sadness, young and old.

Woman's Hour rang, the interview goes out at 10 o'clock this morning.

Had a phone call from an old friend, David, from my past, must be 40 years plus, that was good.

Did a little more painting of Bath Abbey for the charity card.

Felt ok. but very sad. I feel lost and very tearful today but then, I could hardly feel happy, could I?

I have to paint and be creative to get me through all this torment.

Will go for a walk by the castle soon, blow some of the cobwebs away.

How does one get over losing a child! One loved so very much.

Some paper asked if I would go on a web site but explained I was scaling down for retirement.

Day 41
21st May

Very restless could not sleep well, very close and I still get panic feelings. Janet drove me to Birmingham. Sometimes it is good to get away from the places that bring back the memories of the past. We must keep doing things and moving on to a future which we don't have control of at the moment.

BBC. rang about yesterdays interview. It appears many people were moved by it and had rang in or E-mailed the programme, some of they they will forward on to me.

I wish I did not have to do these things but it is important that Caroline should not be forgotten.

The flowers and trees are beautiful now in England, and where Caroline died in Australia, many people are still placing flowers.

The Telegraph rang for an interview regarding students and young people having their gap year. I think back to my student days, I would have liked the chance, but it was not so then.

Day 42
22nd May

Restless night, just thinking and feeling lost. Thinking Richard has no sister now, he is now an only child, no other little family to be close to and have a base.

I will have no Grandchildren, from Caroline, to tease.

Sometimes I hate so many people I should not, drugs and mess have taken my Daughter from me and my family.

Just painting today, need to get something done.

Press from Australia rang, I gave them an interview regarding how I feel about the Police enquiry and the murderer (It were better for that man never to have been born)

That person must be someone's child – as Caz was mine and Marjorie's, and Richard's sister, and always will be until the end of time or until love ends.

Why do I want to go to Australia? Perhaps to make my peace to end a chapter of my life, to paint away the pain in my heart which seems never ending, who knows?

I must follow what is my destiny with strength and honour. For what we do in life must surely echo in eternity.

The gallery. Let's hope for a good offer. People looking around today.

The murderer will have to face what he has done as surely as the sun will rise and waves flow to the everlasting sea.

There are to be many tears and torment not only for the perpetrator of this heinous crime but for the family of the perpetrator of this unspeakable act of mindless aggression against the innocent. Time will be the weapon of defeat for of this, the world cannot forgive or forget. It will be written in the sands of eternity MURDERER you are and always will be. Go walk in the halls of evil and never show your face by day or night slayer of the innocent, prepare for eternal shame cursed be they that protect you for such a cowardly act. Do not call yourself human, just a coward and a murderer of a child. God will take vengeance on your wretched soul. Go walk in darkness and may hell be always at your heels. So is the curse of a father of a murdered child. May your deeds be chronicled in hell, do not for shame sake ask for mercy.

Sarah, the wonderful Police officer, rang with information and tells of condolence book and photographs from Australia. I had a quiet but agonising day, did a little painting in watercolours. Brian rang from Stansted Hall, friends send best wishes, and life goes on. Just want to sleep.

Day 43
23rd May

Slept well, feel ready for doing some painting.

The weather is windy and even some rain, the spring is beautiful even though my heart is so very sad and my life seems so empty now. The pain seems to go on and on, though in different ways and feelings, never two days the same. It is important to keep going and trying to work. Keep stable and life must go on, I don't want to live in the past, I have so much to do with my art not only for Caroline. I do have a son who is also of utmost importance and so many friends all over the world.

I must do the Australian trip and get it done in a respectful and dignified way. Perhaps it will be the last chapter of this little book and the beginning of a new adventure in the future.

Had a good day painting, felt tired more than usual. Went to sleep for two hours or more this afternoon.

The vision still goes on in my mind of Caroline screams and a feeling of need – HELP DAD. Oh God what a future.

Checked E-mails and returned some.

Day 44

24th May

Good sleep, feel a little more rested. It is important to let your body heal in it's own way, listen to your body and you will not go wrong, but keep doing things whether it is cleaning the car or writing. In my case I try to keep painting and talking to people and seeing friends, you make many new ones along the way some who have had similar experiences, regretfully many people have and some worse. Keep going, be brave and only deal with the truth and how you feel.

Remember you have nothing to lose, yet many things to be constructive with.

Janet drove back to York for the Telegraph and Minster filming. All went well, felt rather tired afterwards.

Janet is wonderful, I could not manage on my own now.

When you are going through the death of a Daughter, divorce settlement, problems with the business, it makes you stressed, that is why you need to do something you like every day. Be positive and remember what the person you are mourning for would want.

Video and many letters from Australia at the gallery in Scarborough, too many to list but all very beautiful. I may write about these at some future time. We will see some of the people on our visit to Australia.

I still expect Caroline to walk in through the door. I just can't take it in that she has been murdered. Not little Caroline. Many of her friends are putting flowers on her grave, it is beautiful, people are so good, you can love them all but you don't have to like them all.

Day 45

25th May

Felt rested today, just painted in my Scarborough studio, worked OK but not for too long. Keep thinking of Caroline and her short life, it haunts me, yet in a beautiful way. Not much to say today except it was a good day, even wind and rain can be very beautiful.

Galleries going quite well at present. Janet has been great, I could not manage on my own at the moment and really don't want to.

Heard myself again on the weekend Woman's Hour, it is strange to hear your own voice, any other subject and it would be wonderful. God it hurts.

A quiet day, painted snow pictures, it is very cold in all ways now for me.

Day 46

26th May

Quiet morning, rested though woke up during the night by noise outside. Weather wet and windy but hoped to start The Heart of York painting for Australia to say thank you for all the care that the people have shown

27

for Caroline, will just take it easy and try and relax into it. May not paint any more of this one. There will be a limited edition print of a different Minster picture. It will be called the Australian edition in Caroline's memory. I have thoughts on a special Christmas card for next year, linked to Caroline as a child, to raise monies for a charitable organization.

Went to York, made a few frames, people came to say how sorry they were, must try and work, Caroline would want me to get on.

Saw John at the farm, collected my car on the way back to Scarborough.

Day 47
27th May

A little brighter. Went to the accountants regarding retirement, all seemed to go OK.

Phone call from Italy, would I like to go to Verona for two days, we will see. Why do two days of mess when our countryside is so fresh with greens and beautiful.

Went out for an evening with Brian in York. It was a pleasant evening but strange. I met up with some old friends.

Helped to choose headstone for Caroline's grave, quite hard.

Phone call from Italy, October, not for me. Thinking I may paint in Pocklington.

Just got through the day.

Day 48
28th May

Can't claim anything for sickness, well what did I expect, I have only worked for forty years and paid my taxes up to date etc.??

Went to my gallery in York, all going well.

Felt very tired today, had enough of the blows of life. Rain and wind so did not start painting again.

I should have worked on painting sadly, the weather did not permit. Very frustrated, don't let it happen again. I need to do something positive every day.

Phoned Richard, hope he can come over to Scarborough this week.

Day 49
29th May

Restless night, worry over business and angry over money matters etc.

Dreaming, must be around 5.o'clock, a figure appeared to me, a man with an evil energy, he came through a network of rails, may be a bridge, felt uneasy, it was menacing, he appeared in front of me with a sack over his head, this was the evil energy of the murderer of my Daughter. I shouted out in my dream "you are the murderer of my Daughter, I will kill you". I laid my hands on this energy and awoke, the room tingled as it does even now as I think about that evil energy.

Weather rain and wind, makes a change.

Santa text from Italy, she has had a small op.

News from Germany, all changes there. Janette phoned regarding Jose's health, will send prayers.

BBC. Nicola would like me to do a programme, something for the internet regarding awful experiences. I don't have the energy.

Felt up and down, a little better now that I have done some painting, it helps to clear my mind, must do something positive every day.

What would I do without my mobile phone. Perhaps the spirit is a mobile phone, we can talk, feel and cry. It's been so very beautiful to have been alive with Caroline and she will always live in me as she was flesh of my flesh. Part of me has died with her and part of her will always live on in me for Eternity, though my work will one day decay as will my body, so my love will be eternal and survive death.

Day 50
30th May

Fifty days since my Daughters death. Life goes on and more upset too. Letters from solicitors regarding settlement and business, hardly of any importance now.

Press rang regarding photographs. Press rang regarding prints for Caroline's memory just went with it.

Richard is coming tomorrow, that will be nice. Weather wet and windy, painted in the studio.

Well, it can't get much worse, at least I have my health and my friends. So while we have light I must go on with it but it is hard to keep going.

Painting gives me so much pleasure.

Had nice letters from Woman's Hour. Positive reaction and that is most important.

Halfway day. Bad night. What a mess at the end of a life.

Day 51
31st May

Felt very, very tired today. Started out for York but came back, could not face another wet and windy day to start a new painting, perhaps it will be better next week.

Just needed to be quiet today. It is just like having a continual pain in your heart, and I feel I die a little each day, even though I try to put on a positive stance, because I know If I didn't I would just go down and, for my Daughters sake, I must go on with my work.

Painted in oils today, started a few small ones. Just feel worn out in every way.

Richard came over. I spent the afternoon with him. It was so nice just to have a little time with my son. It is very difficult for him at the moment,

what with the death of Caroline and other problems going on. It's a wonder we haven't all gone mad.

Janet made us a lovely dinner, the evening was all very nice.

Richard may come to Australia.

Day 52
1st June

Weather better today, painted in watercolours. Felt a little more positive.
Went for lunch at the Clock Café with Richard and Jan, very pleasant. It
was so nice to have a bit of fresh air.

Painted in the afternoon but then felt very tired again.

Day 53
2nd June

Weather better, felt better. Just painted a little in watercolours and then
to lunch with Richard and Jan at the favourite Clock Café. All good fun,
it is important to have some fun times to help you to relax and to be able
to talk to people.

Tried to finish off some paintings and started a new one. Things are going
slowly but better.

Lots of people still sending love out to us.

Found out that Mr Jenkins has also lost a daughter, I did not know, he has
my deepest sympathy.

Day 54

3rd June

Going to York to paint the Australia picture. If I go this year or next year I shall enjoy the painting.

Feel more relaxed though the pain will always be there.

Galleries? Just have to cut my losses!

Started painting of York and of course it rained (tears from heaven).

Many people came and gave me a hug and so many people in the same circumstances, children who were killed etc.

Had some lovely letters, one from a reverend in Northern Ireland admiring the ideas I was putting across in the Woman's Hour programme. Very tired.

This evening a beautiful rainbow appeared over Scarborough castle, perhaps a sign of hope.

York gets me exhausted now but it was nice to get outside and paint.

Day 55

4th June

Not a good start to the day, felt depressed and worn out. Going on to York. Had good press coverage but I think that's enough.

Worked most of the day, felt a bit better, work is good for this type of thing.

Feel more rested this evening. Talked to lots of people in York today. Painting started and looking fine up to now. Nature is so beautiful today and at this time of year.

Day 56

5th June

Felt better today, went to York only to find problems with the bank.

Margaret's Sister came over to see us in York.

Gallery doing well but nothing in it for me.

Rain, rain, rain all day, just what we do not need.

BBC. Rang, interview tomorrow, don't know if it is in Australia or UK.

Felt better talking to people and having a bit of fun and a laugh.

Marjorie on the phone, very depressed. We will both be glad when the mess at the gallery is over.

Day 57

6th June

Rest day today. Phone call from the Benefit Office Scarborough. When you are self employed you cannot get help. It does depend on what type of stamp you pay, I will have to get back to them as I have been fully paid up and after the murder of a daughter, financial help would be useful as there are many things to be paid for, I am only painting for therapy, not making any money for the galleries or myself.

(up by the count of nine gives you one second to go)

Phone call from Australia, just a short interview, be positive and get on with life.

The picture for Australia will be predominantly York Minster with it's heart plus the suggestion of a rainbow, flags of both Australia and the UK. and wild flowers in the foreground.

The painting is a thank you to the people of Bunderberg for their kindness and for Caroline's memory.

Thank you from the bottom of my heart, may the sun always shine in your heart and your dreams and hopes come true, from my heart to yours always. Just a Dad.

Day 58
7th June

Felt a little more positive today after a good sleep which is most important. It is important to get rest and relaxation and take an interest in life. There is lots to do although it will never be the same.

Call from BBC. to do a little talk for Scottish region (it is something to do). Went to the gallery and purchased a new folder, got one in the sale, had a few prints done - just a try out. Went out for lunch, quite a good day, it rained a little but did some painting.

Sarah, the Police officer, rang with news about Christa and the Australia link up.

The painting is started and I may even get to go and take it along with Richard.

Feel OK, but need to take it easy sometimes. Writing and talking helps.

Woman's Hour seems to have put the message home. Our future is very much our young people. To think too much of your life perhaps is to lose it!!

Day 59
8th June

Resting time now. Weather a little better now, just going to paint this morning. Will be going back to York on Monday. Decided to paint some seaside fun cards to cheer everyone up.

Went to do some painting but felt too tired. came home and had a sleep instead. Sleep is the most wonderful healer.

Day 60
9th June

Lazy morning but felt much brighter, may have a quiet day.

Went to an event, it was good to get away, outside for a change, although as usual, it rained.

News from the Police that DNA tests are being carried out in Australia with hopes they may get a lead, this brings it all back home just like a knife being turned in your heart. Good after the rain stopped.

You keep thinking of your child in a coffin under six feet of earth, it breaks your heart, but not your spirit. Because that is life and your spirit never dies. I believe we are all parts of God and as such are immortal and wonderful in his eyes.

Day 61
10th June

Another tenth and two months on.

Going to York but the weather is windy and wet as per usual, but even so it is good to be alive.

Many more letters and invitations for TV and radio programmes, news papers etc. all very interested but I must draw a line somewhere as it is very draining to keep dashing here and there. It does not make it very easy for me to start to move on, it is all very draining.

Day 62
11th June

Interview with the BBC. Radio York. Weather wet and windy yet again. Those angels are weeping buckets for me. Will try and get on with the painting.

Feel empty and old but must try to keep positive.

When I pass to that other world Caroline will be there to meet me, the first one.

She was looking at the beautiful landscapes and things of Australia and all she had seen and wondering what heaven was like, the next minute she was there, all the pain forgotten....

Day 63
12th June

Felt funny today, forgetting things, don't know how I can go on in many ways.

Yorkshire TV interested in my book when or if it gets done, also a series of programmes, maybe on art and its power of healing, an important link with being positive and expressing ourselves. Certainly have a problem today with it.

Day 64
13th June

Weather a little better. Had to go to York with a broken tooth, life goes on.

Managed to get on with the Australian painting, the west front of the Minster with poppies, went ok but the weather dull. It always rains when I try to paint, perhaps it is the tears of Yorkshire. Lots of ideas to paint if only the weather would improve.

Day 65
14th June

Rain and windy. Just painted a little and rang a few friends. Stayed in and did a little oil painting. Beautiful rainbows all around me and the sea. Feel tired and worn, had enough in many ways, just feel empty inside and it is difficult to think of what maybe in the future. Weather is foul.

Day 66
15th June

England won 3-0 !!!

A good nights sleep. Painted in the morning in studio, outside in the afternoon. Many people I know or slight acquaintances came to talk to me. Very tired so had to have an afternoon nap, it does you good.

People came into gallery enquiring about the charity. (Foundation needs seeing to).

Doctor's note for a few weeks off has been accepted and perhaps it would be good to have a little less business pressure on me for a change. I have had this for thirty years and feel guilty asking for help, but we all need to relax sometimes, we have paid for it, an old English trait with people my age.

Went out with friends, it is good to have a laugh, perhaps at ourselves. Late night, not used to it.

Day 67
16th June

Fathers Day.

Slept very badly and 'out of sorts'. Gave two radio interviews, Australia and Yorkshire coast, then TV at Oliver's mount. It is a good therapy to get the words and feelings out, yet nothing can take away the pain from my heart.

People have been very kind.

I painted in Hutton-le-hole most of the day. Felt better painting it is a good way of getting the emotions out.

All went well.

Weather very beautiful. Radio & TV tomorrow.

Feel very tired now and still out of soughts. Things have changed for me and my outlook so very much.

The Stream where we paddled in the Yorkshire Moors. Nr Hutton-le-Hole

Day 68
17th June

Robin Hoods Bay today. Spoke to Radio Leeds. Talked to Brian and Mary. Went to find some poppies for Caroline's painting but none to be found. Feelings of panic, don't know how things are going to be in the future. Cleaned the cars, had to do something a bit physical.

Day 69
18th June

Went to York, gave TV interview Radio York and BBC. Look North. Went as well as could be expected, painted outside on the West Front painting. It felt good in the sunshine. The painting is healing and very important.

Found some poppies on John's farm so could sit and paint them into my painting.

Day 70
19th June
No Entry

Day 71
20th June
Richard's Birthday. He came over in the afternoon, a very tired boy, now twenty five, how time passes.

Went out and did some painting. The Endeavour came into Scarborough for a short time, I should have painted it but it was too fast.

The empty feelings and not sleeping, it's a wound that will never heal.

I feel so sorry for Richard, to see him so down hurts and with him staying in that empty house in York, I can not help in any way, he is so alone.

Gave an interview for Australia news, they sound very nice people, perhaps we will meet in Australia.

Brian and Mary came for a meal. Janet made a super dinner and it was a pleasant evening. Talking is good, it puts feelings into words and gets your head in order.

Sometimes I am strong, so strong!

Day 72

21st June

Bad night again. Stayed in Scarborough and just painted.

A pleasant day.

Day 73

22nd June

Bad night, restless. Photo fit news from Australia TV rang wanted full access, sorry not on. The Mirror rang for info.

Recording Radio Five live tonight.

Just did some oil painting.

Jill can't make Stansted but luckyily Jan is over with me.

Day 74

23 June

Went out painting in Scarborough, pleasant weather, and it is better to get out and talk to people, makes you feel better and so does it if the weather is kind and mild.

We went into Filey, very nice to smell the fresh air, feel the breeze and the sunshine, it is very healing in many ways. Painting is very important, it heals with the greens of the grass and the blues of the sky, just to smell the air and enjoy being alive and remembering the times of past joys with the children.

Day 75

24th June

Went to York. Doctors for a blood test, note etc. Lets hope all is ok, blood pressure a little high (hardly surprising).

Worked on painting for Australia, coming together now a little better, feel tired but positive.

Went out with Brian, met up with friends, they were pleased to see me, and want me to get involved with them again.

Need to get sorted and grounded in my work and get all this finished with Marjorie, not forgetting what is mine and all the work I have done over the years, and what I should like from it all.

Weather, of course, bad in York, windy etc.

Day 76

25th June

Spent the day at Hutton-le-Hole lovely weather and pleasant memories.

Came back through Egmont lovely around there and Rosebury, must paint that area at some time, it is so beautiful, and the sunshine was so good.

Painting in Hutton OK, now problem with interview (I forgot) I think it is a sign that I have had enough.

It is nice to have the lighter nights now.

I keep thinking of last year when Caroline was working on her A levels at the college. No one could have imagined what was going to happen this year, in all ways it is a living hell. I really don't care what happens now.

Day77
26th June

Feeling a little bitter and angry this morning. How dare anyone kill my little daughter, it makes me so angry and so very much alone with thoughts in my mind of this distinct evil act, what with all the stupid nonsense going on with the gallery and things going wrong, it is not at all good, plus have had to pay for more funeral expenses, these things certainly bring you down to earth with a bump.

Went out and started a drawing of the Crown Hotel in Scarborough for a complete change and a discipline, It was very windy so did not stay out for long.

Did an interview with the Daily Mirror, they took photographs and all went ok.

Felt better as the day wore on.

Another friend, John came over, what a tonic he was, he really had me laughing talking over old times, it felt good.

Day78
27th June

Phone call from Australian Police.

Many letters from well wishers and one from a lady who heard Caroline screaming and feels guilty that she could do nothing. There have been so many beautiful sentiments made.

Went to paint at the Harbour in Scarborough and then had a little more time on the Crown Hotel drawing.

Interview on radio York about the reward being offered in Australia for information. I would give all my money if I thought it would bring my Daughter back but there is no chance of that. I would not like anyone else to have to go through this torment and, of course, it turned wet and windy, weather disappointing, I feel tired and agitated in many ways, anger at the murder of my daughter. Will it ever go away? Thank goodness for my many friends who have stayed by me in these awful days and will in the days to come.

Rested in the afternoon and then did a little oil painting in my studio.

Just heard of a coach accident and a young girl killed, those poor parents.

Christa informed me that Australia trip around 8th July possible.

Day 79
28th June

Restless night. Drive to York to try and finish painting off for Australia, not a very good day but will do my best. Tears of Yorkshire, perhaps it is true. I have felt concerned about the lady who wrote about hearing Caroline screaming, she must be assured that there was nothing she or anyone else could have done.

Press coverage on painting to go to Australia. It has been a hard painting to do, not one of my best but has turned out reasonably well and should do the job. Will ask Richard to add something to it.

Paid yet another bill, just a little more to go, but will it ever end? I have to try and earn as people need paying. Perhaps that is my life's purpose, I work and earn so others can enjoy spending it!

Day 80
29th June
Beautiful day in Scarborough. I am going to paint.
Just relaxed and enjoyed the day, talked to many people who knew what has happened.

Scarborough North Bay, near my gallery

Press photographs good of painting for Bundaberg and a nice write up.
Felt a little on edge today or out of this world, a strange feeling.
Talked to an old friend Gill on the phone, a good newsy chat. Time goes by so quickly and we must get on with our lives, everyone has something to do, tasks set perhaps before we are born, these tasks have to be done no matter how difficult they may be.
The day was pleasant but still felt tired in the evening.

Packing clothes and paints for Stansted, what a good job Janet is here or I could not cope. Just a feeling of panic at the thought of teaching for a week.

Day 81
30th June

Still feeling empty and angry and missing Caroline. I keep thinking of her inside the bosom of the cold dark earth. It hurts me every day.

Today I work in Scarborough in the morning and York this afternoon, finishing touches to the painting, have now put the rainbow in, and of course it rained. Have left the painting in my studio for Richard to add his bits to it.

My first long drive today back to Birmingham, OK. but very tired. Still have sleepless nights. It all seems so very far away and unreal. It has rained most of the day but I am lucky to be alive.

Getting things ready for Stansted and then maybe Australia.

The painting began in tears and ended in tears, a difficult road.

Must write a few poems.

Day 82
1st July

Restless night, going to Stansted today, it will be both a change and a challenge for me, but I have some very good tutors to help me.

All OK though it was quite a strain going into the college again and getting things going. The usual energy is not there.

It was nice to see some of my students and how they are getting along.

Felt strange but got going with painting and a lecture, it was good to get back to working with the students and they are so kind.

The students worked well.

Day 83
2nd July

Working with the students went quite well, but felt a little tired. Someone talked to me about Italy with a drawing of Santa, what a surprise, talked about Francesca and children, an intuitive lot here, bit of a turn up for the books but all going well even having a little fun along the way, and learnt a lot.

Day 84
3rd July

Working at the college, what a change, felt rather out of things but managed to get back into it, the students were very understanding. It felt strange but good.

It is good to be doing something, but what? Perhaps one needs to rediscover what you really need to do with your life at this time.

One of my students has had a recent heart attack and has not been good, but for his healing he has made some beautiful paintings on a large roll of wallpaper.

Healing through art is very important in physical and mental healing, but so is the will to use colour as a language of the heart.

Painting has always been a language of the inner spirit, very much so for me.

One of the visitors on an earlier course had been taken into hospital, his wife stayed at the college and joined our group, it was most certainly healing for her, plus the added love and care from the students.

I had to face the general public as well as my students. I had to see if I could still demonstrate my craft, all went quite well although I did feel my energy dropping several times, I can do it, I won't resign as a course organiser at the college.

Day 85
4th July

Felt drained, but all the students were enjoying themselves, which is good. It is nice to see them getting a lot out of the course and their art improving.

I find it so important to get on with everyday life in these dreadful conditions. Every day things get more positive.

Managed to paint some of the day, healing for me. If I did not paint I think I would die, if not in body, then in heart and spirit.

Day 86
5th July

Finished off at Stansted. All went fine, but was long enough. Good job I had Jeni and Janet to help with the tutoring, it took a lot of the pressure off me.

Day 87
6th July

Drove back from Stansted. It was a good week and a change of scenery.

Day 88
7th July

A hard night, what with business worries and keeping the bills paid, settlements and most of all the death of Caroline, it's a wonder I don't go mad. I think I do have blood pressure problems.

I just needed to get away and paint today for the healing of my heart, it usually works.

One last heartfelt journey into the blue skies of tomorrow, saying goodbye to yesterdays dreams of grand children from my daughter, Caroline. I now have eternal pain in my heart.

Caroline has done some beautiful lily paintings, I remember doing them with her.

Day 89
8th July
The Australia trip
The hard journey to say goodbye.
Written at the station in York
The start from Scarborough was fine but all was not to go well with mis-understandings and differences of opinion Not a good start. It is not a good thing to have to do. I feel awful, Richard feels awful and Janet is holding things together.

Of course the train is late, no problem, we have plenty of time.

The picture is framed, glass protected, let's hope it can be put on the plane, Peter has packaged it very well, perhaps the last one to do with regard to this matter.

As we sit in York station the crackling of the unreadable voice comes over with the train information, it is very uninspiring. Not a good start to an awful journey.

I keep thinking of Caroline when she went away, all joyful with her friend, Sarah, on a journey that would change Sarah's and end Caroline's life.

Written on the train
Day started well but got worse, misunderstandings etc. weather pleasant but not a good start. Changed clothes at York gallery, met up with Richard.

Got on the train and was covered in spilt coffee that someone had left behind, all over my light trousers, great start.

Things are going to be hard enough but spoilt with harsh words from the onset. This is not ideal. People must learn to pull together when these things happen, not go off in their own world, wanting their own way all the time.

Caroline's Rainbow Foundation set up by Caroline's Mother and Richard is for young people who get robbed, like Caroline, whilst backpacking. It will be for them to get some funds to help them out of a stressful situation. They will be able to contact the Foundation through the Embassy or Police Dept. and it may mean they will be provided with a voucher for an overnight stay in a hostel or the like, whilst things get sorted out.

It is good that both Marjorie and Richard have something to do, in their time of grief and stress, that is of a positive nature.

In stress such as mine there is no solution, it hurts and it gets worse, lack of sleep and business worries, very great pain and loss, bringing with it great mental and physical strain and sometimes people don't help.

In the future, if I dare look ahead I just want to paint in the Yorkshire Dales and please myself instead of trying to please everyone else. The English landscape is so beautiful at this time of year, the greens healing in itself, so many varied greens and the skies. I should be painting.

We speed on to London Kings Cross and then on to Heathrow airport by where I used to live as a student and, for a short time, worked. If anyone then had told me how my life would turn out, well, I would have been tempted to ask for my money back.

I have had 95% of a wonderful life.

Before starting our journey this morning I walked into York and chatted with a few people I know. One of Caroline's friends asked me to say goodbye from him.

Went from the underground to Heathrow, not a bad journey but one filled with anger and bitterness.

We were to be upgraded on the flight but only one made it as the plane was full. We met up with Christa from the BBC. And Keith, the cameraman. In all the confusion Christa mislaid her mobile phone, has not been one of the luckiest days on record but not long to go now until flight.

Written on the plane

Got on the 747, it is huge. Off we fly to Bangkok, Caroline must have been full of it at this point, looking forward to a wonderful adventure.

The plane flies well, lots of bumps at present, must be the clouds (I hope) Richard is more relaxed now, but what can one do or say. It is the hardest thing he will ever have to bear in his life. I am so pleased he was able to come along, it is going to be hard but life can never be easy in any way.

43

We now fly for twenty eight hours, what a very long time.

I have always tried to be correct in what I do, but have not always been correct. It is that we are given only that which we can bear in one lifetime.

Day 90

9th July

(Tomorrow it will be three months)

Slept on the plane, bumpy sometimes, the chart shows us where we are. Tears come into my eyes thinking of the flight Caroline was on a few weeks ago, full of joy going to Australia not sleeping much but chatting most of the time to Sarah.

We are just flying over the Bay of Bengal, Mount Everest, the Himalayas and all that. The flight is a bit lively to say the least, can't write too well, a bit scary. I don't like the bumpy weather, the aircraft wings move so much, but I expect it is all in order.

I need a shave and shower but not too bad.

My sentence and my sadness goes on forever... for eternity.

Changed flights at Bangkok. Just a two hour stop over, another twelve hours in the air.

Caroline and Sarah must have still been busy talking at this stage, full of the things they were going to see.

It is all too awful to contemplate. This reality at this stage in my life that I am now at, what can I say or do? what can I advise Richard to do? How can I heal a broken heart with words? This is going to be the darkest time in my family and in my life, but we must all come to terms, Caroline is no longer in this world but let us hope she is with us in spirit. Only time will tell, we know life goes on as long as she remains in our hearts always.

Day 91

10th July

Still flying across Australia, just looked out of the window and saw Alice Springs. The stars were so clear and bright, we are indeed in another world.

Caroline must have been most excited at this point, we are almost in Sydney, half a world away from England. Altitude thirty-nine thousand feet across the date line and still flying in the dark. What a vast country this is with it's names out of recent and ancient history.

We arrive in Sydney six o'clock in the morning, then on to Brisbane and on to Bundaberg. It feels OK, arriving on the 10th.

We will be staying in Bagara, thirteen kilometres outside the town of Bundaberg.

We were met by the Mayor and the Police at the airport and taken by the Mayor to the council chambers to meet the councillors. They put on a meal for us but we were all really too tired to eat.

I presented the Mayor with the York Minster painting, she was delighted. We arrive at our accommodation, not too long and in bed asleep, had enough and the feelings just won't go away.

Positive feelings make positive energy, it is important to make notes of feelings and the energy around you at all times. This time I am not sure how I feel or what I can achieve with all the thoughts that I have. It is important for all to get it sorted in our mind about all things, all feelings, all thoughts about our lives and loves into the correct perspective and get on with life.

Day 92
11th July

Started painting with Richard at the beach very early in the morning, watched the sunrise. Painting went well, felt the power of the colours, a very definite healing in art. This is all very important.

Could not go to Burnett Bridge as the press were there waiting and we needed to be spared that.

A very busy day meeting people and interviews, the day passed so quickly.

There was a big press conference with all the media, we coped quite well, Richard was superb. I made the official presentation of the painting, the Mayor had presented me with a limited edition leather bound book about the history of Bundaberg.

The tour of the Police station was quite fascinating, the worse part was the incident room where there were pictures of Caroline and her clothes etc on a wall plus the photo fit pictures of people who were being investigated.

Ron Pickering, the Chief Superintendent, was more than willing to answer any questions. If it had not been for the nature of the visit it would have been an enjoyable experience. Richard was given a hat and a badge, they made quite a fuss of him. Ron Pickering is a great person, it must be a pleasure to work for him, if I can say that. But like all the officers working on the case they are giving all the time they can to it as they have taken this so personally and now, meeting Richard and myself, they feel an even closer family. What more of a tribute can I say to them, lets hope the net is closing in on the perpetrator of this awful crime, as they say perhaps only a phone call away.

Richard pleaded for anyone with information to come forward at the press conference which went out on TV, so that should give it more impact.

We had lunch and then to the rose garden where they planted a tree in Caroline's memory. There we met some of the local people who were very kind and again some gave cards and little gifts. There had been a lovely cream tea put on for us. Everyone so generous towards us.

The big shock of the day was when we were requested to meet the acting PM. of Australia, John Anderson, as he was in the area. We had a short meeting with him and then a very short press conference. We have had enough now, we are all exhausted.

Day 93
12th July

The start of another day but the sadness remains. I can feel the sweet winds and gentle sunshine on my face, but my heart cries for what has been done or what has to be done. This is the end of the old world and the beginning of the new. What can I do? Where can I go? The only new is despair the end, if I was a Roman I would fall on my sword and end the eternal torment. The healing painting may be the only thing I can do now. I seem to have destroyed everything that I have had.

I must get on with the next chapter of my life, the first sixty years of my life have been wonderful, two children, a job I love and many dear friends, it ended in a moment of passion, or in my case, stupidity. Is this the journey of life?

The Mayor took us to the Burnett bridge in the evening. Richard and I together again in sorrow, it was if it were planned there was no other person in the world around us and we met, in silence and quiet dignity, on the pathway along the bridge where Caroline had been. Later in this journey we are to walk together along the last journey that my daughter took, to and from the post office where she made her last phone call to England.

The best times have gone, the worst of times are now with us, how can I mourn a lost child? How can this be happening to me? I am away from all the things I have known from now to eternity, here in Australia half a world away lies the body of my daughter still and cold six feet under the English earth. Only the worst torment in my life to come. It's perhaps time for me to end things. I can not find any justification in going on with the way things are, only the old things bring comfort and stability. The things we need are important to any person.

I pray to God almighty, where do I go now?

We all went to dinner with the Mayor, it was a splendid meal and a pleasant evening.

One of the guests gave me a little gift, it was a butterfly she felt it may bring comfort. It was beautiful as it linked Caroline and myself together so very well and the life we shared for those many years together perhaps the end of a beautiful life and experience.

Felt very tired and drained today but had to keep going, it helped to paint a little.

46

Day 94

13th July

Went to the bridge today, the most difficult thing Richard and I have done, but the task has been achieved and all has been done that can be.

Took photographs of the bridge and the area, all looked very beautiful and it was a different way of grieving for Caz.

I can see now why Caroline would have enjoyed this vast and beautiful country.

Perhaps the visit to Burnett bridge in the silence of that early morning on the 13th of July 2002 signifies the end of a part of my life and the beginning of the new, not only for me but for Richard and all the family that I have.

We were taken to the airport by the Police who were and still are working on the case of my daughter's murder. Lets hope it soon reaches a conclusion.

It is the horrendous scream and terror that still haunts my mind and the people who actually heard it, and the desperate running across the bridge and the moments of trauma that ensued when in the last desperate moments of life in this world.

The Police officers told us "It is not just a job, we feel Caroline is our family more than ever now".

This can never be eradicated from my mind and many people throughout this world, it is surely true to say that the death of our Daughter has echoed around the world.

Richard and I had some time to walk around where Caroline was staying with Sarah. In the quiet of the morning it looked so peaceful now, and peaceful is the resting place of Caroline in heart of Yorkshire.

The fresh flowers on the place where Caroline fell is a constant reminder of the love the citizens of Bundaberg feel. I took a little earth in my hand and shed a tear. I will take some to England and sprinkle her little grave with some of Australia.

There were children at the airport with the Mayor. The whole class had done a drawing for us, they thought Richard was wonderful as they think he looks like Prince William, it was great, then they all waved our plane goodbye.

The children are our future.

Day 95

14th July

This day was spent painting and enjoying the wonderful city of Sydney because that is what it is. All day the weather was mild and I started my painting of Sydney harbour bridge, along with the team from the BBC, who have now become our friends and a little family. The unity is wonderful for we have been through al the experiences together, sharing

47

the tears and the dreams, talking of our hopes for future years.

I have learnt much through this pilgrimage, this devastating experience has shown me the true unity of people in despair and an undying love from people's hearts, which you can really feel, tangible, in our very heart and soul.

The hopes and dreams of my son, Richard, are in the very forefront of things now. He will go on to fulfil his hopes and dreams.

Richard made an origami bird which he cast into the sea saying goodbye to his Sister in this world. She will be with him in spirit and dreams, always there to inspire him and to drive him on.

Richard has changed so much with this trip, becoming a man with purpose and destiny in his hands.

During this day I felt very much more relaxed knowing that we had faced our demons of the mind and the fears in our hearts. Now it's eyes ahead, walk forward proud and tall with the future in our hearts and minds. We can only go forward in the hope that out of evil can come good, for I do not wish that any person should tread the pathway that we have had to tread.

The painting of Sydney harbour bridge slowly came to life and with it our hopes for the future, because the span of the bridge joins our world and the world of dreams as the rainbow leads us to our future years and its dreams.

Perhaps our life is a learning, our own special dream, maybe we are only dreams and thoughts, a little bit of God in an eternity of stardust into an eternal cosmos.

As I look at this huge bridge that Caroline saw during the last days of her life, I am humbled by the depth of feeling that I am aware of during this time. I am just enjoying the sensation of being alive to all the elements of nature and the love of our fellow man.

As the days pass and soon the writings will cease on the 100 days of mourning. I sit now and wonder what life is all about. This we may never quite understand in this busy and numbing world. I know my family have become closer and the world's family given us strength and unity, but most of all it has given us love.

Love is the most wonderful power we have in this world and faith that we can go forward with our sense of loss, anger and grief that has also touched other lives as a result of this terrible tragedy. Confronted by our fellow human's hearts, for who can say that we are not touched by a fellow human's loss, and who has not been touched by the hand of fate, be they low or high and during our journey through life we meet all on the campus of humanity, as on this short trip to Australia.

So the day ends with a wonderful meal at Doyle's fish restaurant by the harbour. We laughed and enjoyed being together, perhaps we will never be together again in this way, but I have learnt that we must enjoy the moment. Caroline certainly did and so will I. The future is not always ours but this moment is. Just enjoy being.

I don't like every one but I surely can love them.

We all went to dinner and laughed, please, gentle readers, it is of the utmost importance to laugh and be part of humanity, for laughter relaxes the body and mind and helps disperse our heartache for a short time. So never feel guilty about being with your friends and having a good laugh.

Day 96
15th July

Slept well and felt more contented in some way. All that could be done with honour has been done. We must begin to draw a line and start anew with our hopes and dreams.

Today I shall paint in Sydney and try and finish the bridge.

This evening we go to the airport for our flight back to England, half a world away where the battered body of my daughter lies in the Yorkshire clay. It will take but a few hours compared with the final journey we must all take.

Thence to England's fair shores and gentle rain, from the colours and life of Australia, to write of the things no more as the time and days have now almost past.

Painted all day in Sydney, a good day just spent enjoying myself. Richard went skateboarding, he enjoyed himself which is most important in this situation, he needs to heal himself.

Went to lunch with Jan and Christa at Blues point. Have completed my painting, not a bad picture considering all that has gone on. This is my painting to say farewell to my daughter. Sydney is a beautiful city, lots going on, clean and as some of the citizens say, safe. Of that I am sure or I hope so.

It's good to have finished our journey on a good note. Feel more positive but very tired and drained. We have had an emotional trip, but all has been done with respect. We have also laughed which has been important, fun has not stopped and the laughter helps to heal the heart.

The crew with whom we made the film were first class. Christa producer, director, presenter, travel agent, and general dogs-body for everyone, bless her. Keith, the very patient cameraman who was continually panning, filming and feeding, and Nigel, our top photographer, scout and general man about town. They were wonderful working together. Richard, Jan and myself were also working well together, so all gelled very well.

As I went to the airport I felt very tired and just relaxed in the plane as it flew away to Singapore.

One thing I am sure of at this point. In the days I have spent during these traumatic times, of the feelings and emotions that only a death of this kind can bring about, is that my daughter, conceived in love and loved so much by family and friends, has lived and died not in vain, but leaves this world a safer and better place. Her sacrifice in this life means students of this world, whether they are backpacking or not can do safely. As my son so bravely put it "Let go of your possessions, your life is more important". How brave was that man, my son, for that is what he has become in all this sojourn into the unknown and how brave, the words came from the heart and how very much he loves his sister and the things she has now shown us all.

A life taken away in this manner will never be forgotten by all mankind, but the legacy that she now has given us touches all mankind.

I am so proud to have a son and a daughter like these, taking pride in what they are both now doing. I shall watch them touch the world and hopefully save the life of a young person, or help in a strange way us all to go forward in life, day by day.

What of us, as parents of this horrendous act, we must be braver, our hearts stronger as our strength grows less, is an old saying from the times of the Anglo Saxons. I now write these words as I fly back to England, my homeland, I know these words to be true.

We can never go back in time with regrets and the if only's, it has happened, the unthinkable, the nightmare, it will never go away. It will be the same in a thousand years. As I go on to the end of my life I will never forget my daughter, how could I? I shall keep the memories of her in my heart. The little baby, the laughing child, the fun, the schooldays, trips by the sea, her closeness with nature, and me, seeing things through a child's eye with her. I shall now have a closeness with my daughter that only a few have the privilege to have. I feel the sprit and the strength of her and will see the world anew again, so until I join her in that world of the spirit and while there is yet another day I shall venture with my allotted task working with the only tools I have to ease the pain in my heart, helping others to come to terms with their grief, working with my healing art   looking at the world and using the time to enjoy feeling the sun, and smell the fresh air.

Life is not about collecting material wealth and money, we need just enough for our needs, but the real wealth is inside our hearts, the need for love and understanding for our fellow man.

Caroline is now inside her grave, cold and dark. The gifts we gave her will always remain with her little body as it slowly goes to dust, her spirit will never die, as long as we have the spirit of adventure and hope for our young people's hearts to seek and to explore, to follow their hopes and dreams. This is my hope for the future.

For us all it is the unknown, an adventure or an experience, enjoy the time that you have whether it be long or short, it is of no matter. The old adage says 'It is better to have loved and lost than never to have loved at all' also the saying goes 'live your life like a lion rather than a lamb'.

Fulfil your talents and give yourself a ticket for your aspirations and dreams, it's not length of life it's what we do with it that counts. I remember the immortal words 'we are in Gods hands'. What we do with our life will endure in eternity, this I am sure is true. If we are true to ourselves and our hearts nothing can hurt us in this world or the next. I have tried to abide by this in my lifetime but I don't always make the required standard.

The words Caroline has been murdered in Australia and the sound of her terrified screams will stay with me for the rest of my life. There is no way I can change it or change the pathways of my life in future years to come or indeed the past. The only things I can now look forward to is getting on with my painting, maybe one day returning to Australia, seeing it again through the eyes of my dead child, who most certainly opened a doorway into a new world. I do not hate Australia as these terrible crimes are committed throughout our world.

When the perpetrator of this crime is brought to justice, as he surely will be, I don't know how I shall feel when I see the face of Caroline's murderer. He will have to face up to what he has done and I am sure a severe punishment will be sentenced on him. He will pay in this world and the next. He too is someone's child, their family will suffer as does ours.

There are the exciting things to look forward to regarding Richard and maybe his marriage and possibly grandchildren for me, only in God's good time though.

As I fly back to England this day somewhere high in the sky between Australia and the UK, my mind goes back to the days when Richard and Caroline were young and on our holidays to Greece and Spain, we would ask to see in the pilot's cabin, you could in those days, high above the ground Caroline said "Daddy, we can't see God" and the pilot replied "I hope we don't today"! A classic observation from an innocent child. Now I don't mind when I see God, for I know I shall see my daughter and many friends will be waiting for me. If St Peter says to me "Alan Stuttle, you can not enter in" I shall move him aside and say "St Peter, I have served my time in hell".

As the days pass and the months and years speed by us all, we forget because it is the way of men. I have tried to give my daughters death meaning and hope for the future, but more importantly dignity, for that is all I can do now for her. I cannot see her married with the three children and two dogs etc. and enjoying her chosen career as a criminal psychologist, which would of helped the criminal element most of all.

Caroline will not see me grow old as I undoubtedly will, she will be eternally beautiful and young, I have no doubt that she will inspire Richard and share in his dreams and achievements in future years.

So I shall go forward in my life hoping and praying that our young people are not repressed in their adventures, linking country to country, religion with religion and that some light will be spread over our world and in all our hearts. We can all play our part to make this world a more beautiful place, so lets go forward hand in hand, heart to heart, in love, peace and joy and let the inspiration of Caroline make this world a joyous place for us all. Young people, it is your world now, use your love and power to change it. I am in the last few years of a wonderful life, I hand the future to you and all your wonderful dreams. Never let anyone put you down, always do your very best and aim for the stars you may get the moon.

Love, light and may the peace of your God's love guide you and your heart.

As I fly back to my homeland I cannot help but think of Caroline's body being flown back to her native land wrapped in a shroud all stiff, cold and lifeless with a bruised and battered face which I cannot describe, only stillness and quiet likened to a wax doll, not the energy and life that had left these shores such a short time ago.

The body I saw in the mortuary in York was not my daughter but a shell, the spirit of life and youth had flown.

I know that the best of times for me are over, people change into something that you can't recognise and walk away from things they should not, none of us are perfect, nor can we ever be, I try to make allowances for all.

We are but mortal air and dust...

52

Day 97

16th July

Richard and I have now almost completed our journey to Australia to face what should never have to be faced and dispel any doubts and fears we had of the area in Bundaberg where Caroline was murdered. It was quite beautiful also the campsite where Caroline and Sarah were staying, well kept and of a good standard.

The days pass so very fast but we did what was needed, to face the reality of the bridge and the surrounding area. To think a crime like this can happen there is unthinkable. The locals said this does not happen in Bundaberg.

So many tears were shed for my daughter, it was overwhelming for us both.

We were all looked after superbly by the Mayor and her councillors. All is being done that can be done to catch the criminal, DNA Testing starting to take place, far too much to write about in this short diary. Chief Superintendent Ron Pickering was outstanding, as have been the Queensland police, all so very hurt by this crime.

We were made so very welcome by everyone. What more can be said and some things are better left unsaid.

Yes I liked Bundaberg and would like perhaps to return one day and just paint. Who knows?

I can no way dislike or blame, I mean, regarding Caroline's murder, as the Police say it is just one maggot who will soon be found out and dealt with. What have I learnt about myself? That is all that I can think about at the moment. I do not wish to speak about the involvement of anyone else in this matter. People must do their own thing. Of my son, Richard, I am so proud, he has grown and will surely face the world now as a man. His pathway is open to him and must not be interfered with in any way by anyone. He must also spread his wings, fly and live his life. In future years to come he may, I hope, have children of his own, all in God's good time. Me? Well, I wish to move on and be happy for the time I have left with my family and friends, because an experience like this makes you realise how many real friends you have and have made during the years. I shall dispose of my properties and give away what I don't want, and perhaps stop spreading my wings so much and enjoy the days to come.

My house where we lived with Caroline and Richard, is so sad now, it feels dead.

Perhaps one day it will again ring with the laughter of children, with another family of a younger generation. I do hope so.

When a thing like this hits you it is very much a time for change and perhaps for good. Life for me is like a stream, ever onwards and down to the sea of universal consciousness and eternity.

I shall try not to be bitter and angry, but I expect I will at times, I shall try and learn by my mistakes, but I expect not. One thing I will always know is that, deep in my heart and soul, I have a daughter that the world loves and of who I am very, very proud.

Not everything has worked out in my life but 95% has. I followed my dream at fifteen years old by saying to my dying Mother "I want to go to art school" I did so and made my Mother and Father proud of me. I had two children and I am very proud of them.

We went to Australia with a wonderful team of people from the BBC. It could not have been a better group, they were sensitive and caring, a job more than well done, and Janet, my dear, dear Janet, without whom I could not manage. She has held my hand all the way, what greater love can anyone want than constant care and understanding. I would like Janet and I to go forward together in the coming years. A constant and honest heart, what more do you want.

I know the one important truth; that when we pass from this life we move on to the world of the spirit. What will remain of us is love, and those ties can never be broken.

I have written these ramblings in a diary that Caroline gave me in the year 1999. "To Dad wishing you a happy Christmas and lets hope it is a good 1999. lots of love, Caroline." What has been written in it has been done with love, also a broken heart and many tears. Who could have known then what was to happen in so shorter time.

In thought I can travel anywhere in an instant, in past or present, but in body it takes days.

After a very long emotional and physical journey half way around the world in search of inner peace, if that now can ever be attained, but at the end of this day from Australia on the last leg of this horrific journey, I enter the city of York and feel strangely calm. As a final tribute I stop at Caroline's grave and sprinkle the flowers and the handful of soil from Australia where she fell and died. I was fresh from Australia and brought the thoughts of love and healing from all her friends there, the people she had met on her journey of a lifetime that led to eternity and love, for she has now entered God's Kingdom and no longer feels pain as we feel it. I believe now she is part of the great universal love.

Day 98
17th July

Worked in Scarborough to the sound of the seagulls, Australia half a world away. The weather dull and it had been raining, could this be a dream? I could not be sure.

I feel jetlagged and rather tired. Letters to answer and things to do with everyday life. The day was difficult with the long journey and meeting people, it took it's toll on my energy.

Did some painting in the morning and slept in the late afternoon. I'm half in Australia and half in England.

The journey of a life time done in a short but very hectic week.

Day 99
18th July

And on to York, my beautiful city and so much a part of my family and my life. Personal matters now have to be sorted out, my gallery in Micklegate, all this needs my attention. It has been important all along the way to keep working and doing. I believe that if you sit and go deep into yourself it would become very difficult to move on with your life because that is really important.

My daughter spent her short life doing things and so have I because experience is a wonderful teacher and we came to this world to learn something and understand ourselves. We are always in the right place at the right time, our choices are often made for us and the people we meet are of great significance to us. The teacher will come when the student is ready, this is so very true. It is what we make of it all is what counts. I drove to York and walked the streets I know so well and have painted so many times throughout my life, I felt strongly a peace, more settled than I had been for some time. I met many people who came and hugged me or shook my hand because many knew the pain of my loss, friends, partners, husbands, wives but thank God, not too many children. I pray God that no one has to be where I am now. It was good to feel that unity of love and caring.

Many had seen the programme from Australia with Richard and myself, many said it gave them strength and hope, that is what we wished to do. I am so proud of Richard.

My family and friends all over the world gave us so much love and help throughout and continue to do so. When you are in need you find out who your friends are, you can be given quite a shock in that direction.

I worked on a watercolour I started before Caroline was murdered. It is important that life goes on. Felt the sun on my face and the handshake of friends and people that I have known over the thirty or more years.

It pleases me that my daughter and son have touched the hearts of so many people throughout the world. Today I am proud that we have two very special children.

Another murder on the Isle of Wight of a young girl age fifteen, my heart goes out to those parents, I pray for them.

Day 100
19th July
(At an end)

The last day of this diary, kept with tears and love. After this day I will write in this diary no more. I shall write of different things, of childhood through Yorkshire, through my paintings and of the friends that I have met along the way. This diary has inspired me to continue writing. It has helped me a great deal with my grieving. You have to do something, write, paint, dig the garden, laugh, cry or go for long walks but always know that your loved one is always with you, forever in your heart and mind as their spirit lives forever. You can kill the body of a person and they may, like a ripe fruit, fall from the tree of life, but the spirit will go on forever, and we will all, one day, be part of that universal consciousness.

What have I achieved by my journey and my writing, the tears, pride and joy of this journey in my diary? Well! I feel now the beginning of an inner peace and joy for my daughter's life, because she filled her life with sixty minutes fully run, filled her life with her dreams, was always doing something with her many many friends, what more could I ask as a father. I am now and always will be so proud of both my son and daughter. Caroline lives in Richard and Marjorie's heart always, and they have been very brave. We all have to face our bereavement in our own way, this has been my way, being as positive as possible, through the healing with my paintings, the colour, and with the writing, expressing my feelings in this way has truly been healing for the mind, body and soul.

If you had told me a few weeks ago that our daughter would be murdered in Australia, and that my son and myself would visit Australia, that the whole world and people would give us so much love, I would never have been able to cope or handle anything like this, a nightmare unbelievable. What has indeed helped is the heartfelt love and support from all over the world, it has lifted us when we could only have fallen, we send them our eternal thanks. Nothing can give us back our daughter but Caroline was a very positive young lady and through her spirit many things have come out and this makes it very positive, this can only grow.

My belief is that the spirit survives the body and continues it's journey in another world, this belief has helped me a great deal, this is an important part of my teaching. I think this must be spoken of because I have travelled to many countries as an artist and am aware that I am inspired by the power of the spirit.

One of the many things in this book of one hundred days that has given me proof of a universal mind consciousness, was the gift of the butterfly given by the lady in Bundaberg at our dinner with the Mayor. It is beautiful in gold with coloured stones, she could not have known that Richard and Caroline loved nature and we used to hatch butterflies in the greenhouse in our garden at our house in York. One morning in early July, I said to Caroline "The chrysalis is ready and the butterflies will hatch soon, so keep a close eye on them". I go into the house to get things ready to take her to school, when a delighted cry from Caroline came

"I've seen it! I have seen the butterfly hatch!" and indeed she had. In all my sixty years I had never seen it. She was so full of joy to see something that daddy had always wanted. She was a delightful child. It was my privilege to walk her to school when she was in the infants in New Earswick. This gesture from a stranger made me tingle, she said "Something just told me to give it to you, I don't know why". It is up to you what you make of it but there are many things that we do not understand. I write this last page in Scarborough. The gulls cry and I can smell the sea and feel the sunshine, it gives me strength. I think of the past weeks and of Caroline's last visit to Scarborough in February 2002 before going to Australia, when we walked by the sea and had a photograph made and I said I was so proud of her and what she was doing. My little girl had grown into a beautiful young woman and always will be.

When at the age of five we walked in the snow at my friends farm at Flaxton and looked at the tracks of the rabbits and all manner of animals in the snow she said in her five year old voice "Daddy, I could walk with you forever", as she held my hand, and in many of the following years we had many bike rides and walks together along those same lanes, but that memory I remember so well, she was so very young.

When she was young I would collect seeds of all types including acorns and horsechestnuts we would plant them and many would grow, much to our delight. I still have three of the small trees that we grew, they are in pots, very shortly I am to take them to John and Angela's farm, where they are to be planted out along a new driveway, these will be for Caroline's memory, they will grow there for the next fifty years or more, and some other little girl will collect the seeds and plant them and Caroline's memory will live on in another child's joy.

As the one hundred days come to a close, the final thing we must do is to write the epitaph for the tombstone. What should I say? I don't know as yet and it is not all up to me. I think as I dedicate this diary that Caroline gave me in 1999 the last year of the old millennium. To Caroline with love from us all or just with love.

We must go forward in this new millennium as Caroline, our beautiful daughter so bravely did and her spirit always will.

Pray God have mercy on the soul of the murderers of all such children.

Chapter Three

I last met with Caroline on the 6th February to buy her rucksack and other essentials.

She was really looking forward to it, we had a quick coffee and said goodbye as she was rushing off as usual.

Her trip of a lifetime was starting on the 9th February. I said I would not go to the station as there would be enough people there waving her off and crying. She promised to Text and E-mail me and that was great by me. She kept her promise and I don't know how anyone could write so much on a small postcard, she managed.

Text 7th February
Thanx Dad have a good time in Italy and things I'll e-mail you from Oz. Lots of love Caz.

First e-mail was a Hello from Sydney 16th February.
Have been to Bondi beach just as you imagine, have been to the aquarium to see the sharks and crocs. Have seen the koala's and kangaroo's at the zoo have been to the highest point in Sydney and seen the night views around the harbour and the opera house.
Hope all ok with you keep me updated on what is going on there. I'll be in touch soon. Love Caz xx

Postcard arrived shortly after again talking about Sydney, getting over jet lag etc. seeing the bridge and the opera house she says 'pretty incredible' and gives me her new mobile number so I can text her.

22nd February e-mail
Thanx for your e-mail, we are still having a lovely time it is getting hotter and hotter! Wearing plenty of sun cream so I don't turn into a crisp as you put it.
Saw koalas today and had a camel ride on the beach, at a place called Maquarie it is quite nice here till thurs. then moving up coast.
I'll be in touch soon
Love Caz xx

Postcard from Byron bay, lovely place people really friendly great beaches where we are having our surfing course it is brilliant I can stand up now. Weather mostly hot and sunny. Seen dolphins and had a camel ride which was fun.
Hope you like the postcard got one that looked nice for you to paint.

7th March e-mail
Thank for the e-mail. It will be nice for you in the Dales, hope it doesn't rain! I know me and Judy had a lovely time when we came with you.
The surfing lessons are going well, some funny photos, mainly of us falling off.
Haven't seen any more wild animals except a big guana which is like a iguana. Seen a few butterflies but when we move further up the coast we might see some wild crocs.
Still having loads off fun.
Hope you got the postcards. Lots of love Caroline x

20th March e-mail
Hi Dad
Thanx for e-mail, glad you liked the postcard I'll keep sending them to keep you informed on what I'm up to and where I am. I've taken loads of photos so you can see them when I come home.
This morning we got up at 5 to go and see the sunrise, the lighthouse is the most easterly point in Oz so we are the first people in the whole world to see the sunrise.
Here for another week then moving further up the east coast. Booked a really nice sailing trip around Whitsunday island and a 4 x 4 safari on Frazer island too. I'll tell you all about it when we've done it. Be in touch soon lots of love Caz xxxx

1st April my Birthday and received a card and a postcard again full of information with a balloon and a birthday cake with candles drawn on it by Caz.
Hi dad firstly happy birthday, hope this gets to you in time (it did) still having the best time ever. Moving on to Brisbane soon, may do some work fruit picking. We have met up with some friends from England seems a bit weird meeting people you know over here. We have still got loads to look forward to sailing trip 4x4 safari and diving in Cairns so am looking forward to loads. Have a great B.day. I'll be in touch soon Lots of love Caz xx

Postcard
Hi dad hope you are well and had a nice Birthday. We have now left Byron Bay and moved further up north. To surf here is paradise. It is very hot here but been fun so far. Have been to a massive shopping centre which was fun tomorrow to a place called dream world a big theme park so that should be fun and something different to what we have been doing since we arrived here in Oz. Next stop Brisbane. Still having loads of fun Lots of love Caz x

Text 6th April
Glad you liked the card. We start work tomorrow fruit picking, anyway I'll keep in touch. Lots of love Caz xx

That was the last contact I had with Caroline. These Texts, e-mails and postcards will always be precious to me just as precious as she was to me.

I wanted to share these very private words to show others what wonderful experiences can be had by travelling our world, I can feel the joy in her words, the happiness, the fun and the thrill that my Daughter was having on here adventure of a lifetime.
I told her it would be the time of her life, how true this came to be.

In her bon - voyage card I wrote ' Caroline go for your dreams. One of my dreams was to have a little girl like you, my dream came true. Have the time of your life. Love always Dad XXXXX

North Bay 2004 - the beach where we played

Chapter Four

Richard's tribute

The Pilgrimage for my sister

Looking back over this last year I now find myself wanting to speak of a very emotional and stressful trip to Australia. We went to build up a relationship with the police in Bundaberg and hopefully help the case for my sister by way of an appeal. I kept a week long journal and hope parts will portray the emotion and sentiment of Australia.

We embarked on our journey three months to the day when my parents were told the devastating news in the UK. and I received a four am. call in the French Alps. After two months of chaos and disbelief, one month of not understanding who, why and what the hell was going on, I find myself on a plane next to my father with not enough leg room, its strange how life goes. After I'd worn out the in flight entertainment I had a lot of time to think.

Comparing myself to her, remembering situations she and I had been in and how lucky we were, all the time truly believing that MY family were immortal. Shit happens but always to someone else. "They say people who die young live fast lives, its true she was always busy, something happening all the time. All I seemed to be doing at the time was chilling with my mates, having a tipple in the pub or at work."
As we flew over Alice Springs at about four in the morning all I could see from the window was a circuit board of lights, then darkness in every direction. It was sinking in that Cas would have seen the same only six months earlier. "Caroline's Rainbow Foundation. That is her new form in this world; she will be in our hearts forever."

Thirty six hours in the air and we finally arrive in the small airport of Bundaberg.
As we were driven to the Mayor's office I remember the world spinning, it all was too much for my mind.
Meeting the councillors was crazy, we presented the picture dad and I painted of York. We had a drink and a bite to eat.

We were staying at a B&B in a place just up the beach called Bargara, the owners are British and were from Selby, a town near York. It became a welcome retreat, taste of home for the few days we stayed.
Six am. we were up and on our way to the beach to watch and paint the sunrise. Seven am. our thoughts were to head for the bridge, when we

checked it was crawling with cameras and reporters, so knocked it on the head and went back for a welcome breakfast.

9.30am. we were picked up by the police and the real pressure and reality of it all started. Down the station the chief superintendent showed us the whole facility including the murder investigation room for Cas's case, meeting the whole team who were working far beyond their duty, putting in many hours of free time. I had a lot of confidence in what I saw and what they were doing.

Next in our busy days schedule was the press conference, my heart was pounding dad was speaking very emotionally. I was blank, after a deep breath and asking Cas for help I spoke about the foundation how its going to help and hopefully prevent tragic circumstances such as ours. The chief super leant to me and asked if I could make an appeal for anyone with information to come forward, looking back I was surprised how clear it all came over.

After lunch we were due at the botanical gardens where a tropical beech tree was planted nine days after her murder, the tree was planted in a beautiful spot by an amazing lake. The press were all over the place but by this point I was learning to ignore them.

We were driven from the gardens straight to a meeting with the MP. for Bundaberg and Australia's acting Prime Minister. He told us how his sister was killed in a sporting accident, so could identify with what I was doing and some of the pain I experienced. Another press conference and back to police headquarters for a live radio chat. We were both flagging by this point the day was nearly over, back to the B&B for a welcome rest.

After a bad nights sleep we were down by the bridge by 6.30am. Dad and I wept, it was the hardest moment of my life, words cannot express the sadness the loss, loneliness and emptiness I was feeling and also the longing for her back, deep down knowing it was the one thing I could not have. Not only at that moment it is every hour, every day of my life, I miss her more than life itself. The saying you don't know what you've got until its gone is more true than I ever realised. My Dad and I walked around the campsite and paced the last walk of Caroline's short little life.

As we were leaving Bundaberg bound for Sydney the Mayor was there to see us off along with some children from a local junior school, they gave us a wonderful card that they had made and a hat and teddy bear. It was a very touching moment for us and a great memory of Bundaberg.

Situations like this can happen anytime in any part of the world
I would love to experience Australia under different circumstances.

Brian's tribute

Nightmare

We all experience dreams, and when the dreams are not pleasant, Nightmares. We go to sleep secure in the knowledge that if we should have a nightmare, we shall indeed awaken and all will be well. Well perhaps. This year 2002, in April, we who we knew as Caroline (Cas) Stuttle experiences a nightmare of epic proportions.

I was roused into my nightmare when my friend Alan (Caroline's father) rang me at 8.00am.wondering what was the matter He said "its Caroline, she's been murdered"
I went as quickly as I could to be with him and was shortly followed by Jan and many others who offered a great deal of support for Alan in his trying time.

I was with Alan when he went to see the vicar to arrange a funeral for his little girl.
At that funeral I was honoured to be able to speak about a lovely girl who I first knew as a precocious pre-teenager.

Caroline had always been full of ideals and ideas. She wanted so much from life and was prepared to go out and get it. It was this that was her undoing. She went on a backpacking holiday around the world. She went with the blessing of her parents and with their full support. Having reached Australia and had many adventures was intending to go fruit picking in Bundaberg with friends in order to get some money together. Following all the rules she went to phone her boyfriend in England. On her way back to the camp site where she was staying she was brutally attacked and murdered for a handful of change.

I have seen the nightmare unfold and I have seen my friend Alan, have the life drawn from him and slowly with much assistance rebuild his life. I saw a lonely plot of ground where the body of a beautiful young viva-cious girl was laid to rest. I have seen the human spirit manifest itself and become a powerful weapon against the evils of this world.

Alan started to enter the details of his days in a diary. He intended to write for a hundred days as a memorial to Caroline and as an aid to those in similar circumstances. His hundred days are up. He has reached a point where he stopped writing but for him and for us all, the nightmare continues.

For me the nightmare continues, as it does for Caroline's family and friends. The dream is that we can live our lives safely and well but the reality does not always allow that to happen. What we must all of us do is to insist that we live the dream. Our nightmare may never end but lets hope for those who follow on will not experience the nightmare as we have. Let them have a full and rich life free from dangerous dreams and the terrors of the night.

To Caroline we send our heartfelt good wishes. We wish her God speed on her journey through the New Life that we know she is now enjoying.
Sleep tight with no nightmares at all
Safe in the hands of Angels

Brian Gledhill MSNU.

Chapter Five

I have always admired poetry and for many years have written words on impulse reacting to that which has inspired me. All of my old diaries hold words some in verse some in prose of my inner most thoughts, also those which this tragedy has urged me to write. So here I share some that seem appropriate for this very significant chapter in my life.

Caroline was born 2nd September 1982

Written 22nd August 1982

Thoughts on a child
Inside a womb there lives a life unknown to me yet loved
Inside a womb there beats a heart unknown to me yet loved
Inside of me there beats a heart that needs this love unknown
Inside of us there lives a need to know this love unknown.

Written 1982 on seeing a child feeling absolute terror on TV.

The eyes of a child looked into my soul
Why so much terror there?
My eyes began to fill with tears
My wretched soul was bare.

Written 2nd June 1990

IF
IF only a hand would show me the way
IF only a light would guide my steps
IF only I had said yes and not said no
IF only I had followed my heart and not my head
IF only my heart could feel no pain
IF only I could start from the beginning again
IF only the stars stayed still in the sky
If only my God would let me die.

Written 14th April 1993 inspired by some Tibetan teachings

10 Commandments to myself
1   Emblems are worn in the heart not on it

2   The world is wonderful and so are the they that are upon it
3   Hatred can blacken the heart only love can make it whole
4   Be not a burden to any man lest yourself needs a prop to stand
5   Be wholesome in your heart and mind lest you are found wanting
6   Be always of good cheer as things always work for the best
7   Man must live in harmony with nature and himself lest he looses his
    way
8   He that has strength has power to help the weaker soul
9   Be ever confident know that I am always near speaking truth into
    you heart
10 As you breathe sweet air into your nostrils I will breathe knowledge
    to you

Written 1998

The Young People
The young people that I have known are now old and grey
Yet my paintings stay as they are
Quietly the years pass over them but I must fight the last fight
Strike the last blow against the on coming of time
I stand still and take the blows of time until time itself says yield
Though I shall be drunk with blows
I shall stand and have a last chance with change.

Written 4th May 1999

In the valley of my mind there is such sorrow there
In the darkness of my heart there is such a load to bear
Take the darkness from my mind cut deep into my heart
For in the darkness of my soul is such a need to part

Written 2002

Better
It is better to walk this world alone
Than to take on the burden that breaks your back
Deadens your mind and breaks your heart
For in the end we arrive alone are born and die alone.

Life is like a passing cloud you see it and then its blown away.

High above the clouds our problems are as small as ants and we can see the vastness
of our projects and the windows of our mind, for god sees us by standing away and we see ourselves by sitting inside

Written 8th July 2002

My last gift to you
What gift can I give to my dead child
I would that I could give the gift of life
The life we gave you has been cruelly taken away
By a horrendous cloud a fall and then unending sleep
Would that we were there to catch you as you fell
But Jesus caught your soul and took you into heaven
Your sunshine face has gone from us but always lives in my heart
My last gift to you is love your gift to me memories of happy days
Your gift to us an eternity of smiles

Written 9th July 2002

A Rainbow in the Sky
Three months ago you flew through the skies
The same skies that I now fly
Three months ago you were destined to die
Not before you flew through this sky

Three years ago you were here with us all
Three years ago no problems at all
Just going to college just enjoying life
The life that was ended that dark dreadful night

Three continents now I fly overhead
I fly to places you knew before you were dead
Murdered in a place you loved so dear my eyes fill with tears
I shall never see clear.

You were in Australia that I go to now
With Richard you brother close to you now
With tears in our hearts that can never be healed
We go shed our tears in a Bundaberg field.

Written September 2002

The sun has shone on me today
But not on you
The flowers have bloomed for me today
But not for you
My heart has lived today
But not for you.

Written 2003

The first
The first snow has fallen
The first rain has kissed the grass
The first new grass has shown its head
The first year has past
The first blossom fallen
The first sunlight risen
The first swallows flown away
The dreams that should have been
Have all turned to dust in my daughters grave
That should not have been.

Written March 2003

A year ago the world changed for me my dreams for you were dashed
A year ago your bright young heart was full of hopes and joy
A year ago you walked in sun the wind was in your hair
A year ago your life was cut before you were aware
A fathers love is always there for you forever more
Perhaps one day we all shall meet and laugh on that forever shore.

Written 2003

The silence is present....
We can not hear it....
But simply feel its mortality....
Forever the silence is waiting....
To return.... To the present....

A last goodbye

So this is it

The ending of a time, my gallery closing, the vibrancy of life is quiet now, the silence of thirty years has fallen on my studio.

The early morning birds sing, they herald the beginning of a new day.

What is the end of my creative is a beginning for someone new.

All I can leave is my dreams, the paintings I have made in this very room are etched on the wings of time, and like me can never return to their creative past, long may it be so for this is the way of things.

From this place I take my unremembered dreams as the mists of time shall give forgetfulness.

Me! Well I shall dream again perhaps in another place I have not yet dreamed of .

As long as I have light my life shall continue.

We must all tread the roads of future dreamlands.

Written 19th July 2002

The end of a chapter

What do we say? What do we feel? When feelings and tears have been so close. For this past time of one hundred days we have learnt to be in despair, to cry and to measure time which seems to go slow… an eternity in one hour… and one hundred days a billion years… yet my heart is still beating and I must go on with my life… and shall……………………..

Chapter Six

19th February 2003

8.00am. Phone call from Australia, the end of the investigation may be in sight, an arrest may be imminent. Thank god for all the hard work everyone in Australia has done, they have put all their feelings and heart into getting a positive result.

The Australian police have never slackened the pace of their work during these past months, we have the utmost respect and admiration for them all. Both police and public alike. All me and my family can say is a heartfelt thank you from the very bottom of our hearts.

Our beautiful daughter can never be brought back to us but will always live in our hearts as long as we ourselves have life. She was laid to rest by the people who loved her and whom she also loved in the county of Yorkshire her home for nineteen years.

I, as her proud father, kissed her head and held her cold hands in her coffin shortly before it would be closed from the light of the world for eternity. Never again would she feel the sunlight nor breathe the fresh air of summer and would never enjoy the sweet adventures of life.

I would dearly wish that no other parent would have to bear this burden of losing a child to the vicious act of MURDER. For what? a mobile phone and a few hard earned pounds on the adventure that was to cost her dearly.

Caroline was a child who would never do any harm not even to the smallest insect never mind another person.

I visit my daughters grave, though I know that her spirit has long since left her body. I feel tears, anger, and utter despair on going to that place. Why? What for? Who would do such a thing as taking the life blood of what was really just a child enjoying the world. Here only silence, no sounds of Dad as she used to say, I will never hear those words again from her now dead and blooded mouth, never to speak again, her eyes will never open again and smile. "HI DAD" she was always such a joy and I am so proud of my daughter. To see her now - her beautiful clear eyes will decay and turn to dust in the cold unforgiving grave she was sent to sixty or more years before her time. Would I, if I could take her place? I would gladly do so, and so I believe would any other parent.

My life is like a living nightmare that never changes its face by night or day. Whatever I do, wherever I go the pain is always with me. Night and day for always and eternity in her grave lies part of me.

I will never see her children, my grandchildren, I shall never hear them laugh or cry. All I can hear is the scream as my daughter fell or was thrown from the bridge in Bunbaberg, and feel the terror in her heart as she was pursued by God knows what creature or thing from hell to which it will surely return for judgement by a higher will than we will possibly know.

Her screams were heard by many people, yet went unheard. Those who reported the scream say it was of pure terror, something of the like that they had never heard before. Perhaps not of this world! Some say it can still be heard by people crossing the bridge seeking for that which is lost, the innocence of a young life destroyed by a monster.

May God have mercy, and pray that the perpetrator of this crime has the conscience to endure its punishment.

20th February 2003
The perpetrator was apprehended and charged. Now the end is with us, now we must make a beginning.

When I look into the eyes, perhaps the very soul of my daughters murderer, what shall I see? What shall I feel. For it is written that this I shall have to do. Will I see a monster, an evil spirit or the fear of a child awaiting the judgment that is so surely to come with measured steps coming to seek retribution for that which has been perpetrated on an innocent child.

The pain in my heart for my murdered daughter will never end. It will go with me to my grave. Part of me died that day 10th April 2002. The pain, the loss is more than anyone can bear, it is an empty feeling, a nausea every day, will it get worse? Every day things remind me of her as a child, a butterfly, a colour, a song.

We must love our children, take them to our hearts, correct them when they are wrong and praise them for doing right. They are our future. Living in the future times to come with the murder of my daughter when half of me lies in the cold bosom of the earth, the rest of me must go on. I must celebrate the life, joy and love which has been given so freely to me in the years that have gone, let us celebrate the years in the sun to come with harmony and peace in our heart. Perhaps one day forgiveness may come. First I must learn to forgive myself for my weaknesses and just allow time to heal.

To be a father is a special gift from God. From the moment of conception and from the moment of birth, I believe the child was chosen by God for you. It is a universal treasure, never to be taken lightly, to be enjoyed always be their life long or short. Enjoy your moments in the sun together, memories never fade away but remain always in your heart.

A book of remembrance was forwarded to me from the citizens of Bunderberg expressing their own personal thoughts. There are three hundred and seventy five individual messages each one a touching tribute to Caroline, some just said sorry.

To finalise this chapter I have selected one contribution that I feel echo's my own personal thoughts as touched on briefly within this page.

Written by Roland Anderson
Caroline our love and prayers are with you now.

Words penned by Reverend Ted Nobbs (1926 – 1995)
I am a child of the stars, my religion, like the clothes I wear will one day belong to the dust of the centuries. My spirit is immortal and belongs to the universe.
Our sons and daughters are the princes and princesses of an eternal kingdom. They inherit the riches and resources of this planet for a span until they continue their journey through time and space.

Chapter Seven

From Helen Anderson
Bundaberg, Queensland, Australia

18th April 2002

To the Stuttle family

I enclose a book of remembrance wherein the citizens of Bunbaberg have expressed their thoughts and feelings during our vigil for Caroline. Many people were too distraught to include an entry in the book. Others left floral tributes with cards. The cards and other tokens will be forwarded to you under a different cover.

A wide cross-section of the community paid their respects to Caroline. I particularly remember the mothers of backpackers and their concern and grief for your lovely young daughter.

Backpackers from all around the district came to pay their respects to Caroline. Many wept openly and some lit candles. Others sat quietly in prayer.

Stewart is a recent arrival in Bundaberg. He is a young man who is deeply effected by Caroline's loss, and intends having a plaque placed in Caroline's memory.

Your warm and thoughtful reply to the mayor, has touched all those who have read it. A copy of the of the letter accompanied a gracious wreath of flowers. The flowers are laid by a simple white cross bearing Caroline's name.

The sensitivity of the media and the investigation team has been commendable at all times.

Randall, a young aboriginal man, performed a special traditional ceremony for Caroline on behalf of the Australian community. Randall relit a white candle which I'd been unable to keep going for his ceremony. The candle burned brightly for the remainder of the day in spite of the breeze.

A minister of religion and his wife (visiting Australia from Southampton) told me they would like to contact you when they return home to England.

There are many incidents which I could recount for you.

In closing, please allow me to convey my deepest condolences to all the family and your friends.

If for any reason I can be of assistance to you, please feel free to contact me.

Your sincerely

Helen Anderson

Amongst the messages contained in the remembrance book are many from young children some as young as six, simple words and sincere.

I am not favouring any one message as all are treasured, I am dipping into just a few .

Words cannot express the shock that all of Bundy felt when this happened, Caroline will never be forgotten by Bundaberg – our thoughts and prayers will be with you always. *Stephen Bennett*

To the Stuttle family and friends
It's shocked us all when this tragic incident happened. I am an eighteen year old backpacker close to Caroline's age and so it hit home really hard. She was a beautiful girl and it's a shame that anyone has to go through what you are going through, and to Sarah, remember the good times with her. Our deepest condolences.
Lindsey & Simon - Canada.

I feel ashamed that we could not guarantee the safety of your beautiful daughter- your loss is so great- I can't imagine. Please forgive us. May your daughter's soul rest in peace.
Many regards Michael, Beth, Mitchell and Jessica.

Not all Australians are monsters. With an eighteen year old daughter wanting to travel to the UK. after completing Uni. I hope to God she is "able to fly". My family sends their heartfelt condolences to you and your family and also hope for a better and safer world for our children.
Ray, Margaret & Katrina Potter

To Caroline's family in England
With the deepest sympathy from :- the grandson of one of Bundaberg's founding fathers FREDRICK BOSS (whose name appears as a council-lor on the plaque of the opening of this bridge 1900) (BOSS-ROMEO-KAFFKA)
John Kaffka – noon 16/4/2002

Cherished
Angel
Robbed
Of
Life
Innocent
Nobodies   (Cleverly using Caroline's name)
Enemy   *Joel, Michelle, Jayden, beau. XXXX*

To the Stuttle family
Caroline is a beautiful English rose who will live in our hearts forever
Rob Messenger

To Caroline's family
This should not have happened to your beautiful daughter, she was an innocent traveller who was enjoying the world as her playground. She will be missed sincerely and immensely by the citizens of Bundaberg. Not all people in Bunbaberg are like this. We are thinking of your family and her friends.
Love Emily Jones & Jenna Joyce XXXX

* I find it very heart warming yet at the same time very painful to read these messages, I relive the agony each time. I find it hard to appreciate the amount of love and support that has been sent our way. The kindness in this world from complete strangers does give us hope for a future world of more compassion and less greed and hate.

As I move on into reading some of the two hundred plus cards and fifty plus letters (the same amount if not more to Caroline's Mother & Richard) **I must include another from Queensland.** This came via the British Consulate Brisbane...

Further to our conversation this morning, as promised, I herewith enclose my book of poems, Poems of the Millennium and the poem titled "A Bridge at Bundaberg", can be found on page 11.

Would you please convey to Mr Stuttle my truly deep sympathy at his loss, as I am a father and grand, in these tragic father myself and admire the brave attitude adopted by him and his family, in these tragic

circumstances.
With kind regards
Very sincerely yours
Trevor LaBrooy

A Bridge at Bundaberg

A crescent moon riding high
 belies the base thoughts of man
Scheming in the fastness of dark
 with innocence roaming abroad
All unknowing and unassuming
 thinking of home and loved ones
A visitor in a land of plenty
 naught but peace in her heart
The excitement of fresh adventures
 things to do and faces new
Security of companionship
 and many a mile to travel
Nary a hint of danger
 lurking ever near
The constant in a rosy world
 shielded and obscured
But always the demon
 plotting and scheming
Seizing any chance
 when caution hid her face
And suspicion lay elsewhere
 Masked by surprise.

Thus, on a lonely bridge
 the killer struck
A poor young girl the victim
 alone and terrified
Her desperate pleas for help
 heard but not answered
Cries of anguish all to no avail
 robbery and murder unfolds
The victim callously pushed
 to fall to her death
No other reason but greed
 a brain explosion
Triggering a manic impulse
 and all for what?
To satisfy a sudden whim
 for money, drugs or lust
But in the end
 a poor girls life
The supreme stake
 and a mindless coward
Stalks the streets unknown
 Ready to strike again.

On the 10th April, 2002, a young British tourist was killed
in Bundaberg Queensland,
when she was either pushed or fell off Burnett bridge.
The culprit responsible for her death at the time of writing
is still to be apprehended.

* I now can report here that someone has been apprehended and is awaiting trial.
As previously mentioned the huge amount of mail we received, with thoughts, prayers, support and love.
Some of the places as well as numerous from England, Scotland and Wales.
Obviously Australia, but also, America, Brussels, Canada, Dubai, France, Germany, Holland, Italy, Spain, Switzerland, Tasmania and New Zealand.

It astounds me to realise how someone so very precious to me, my lovely Caroline, has made the world and the passing of time so small. Not only as I mentioned letters and cards world wide but especially those closer to home and back to my childhood memories and onward.

From Scotland

Dear Alan,

I know my sister Joyce has already written to you, but from me, I wish to express my sincere condolences to you and your family at the sad loss of your daughter Caroline in Australia.

I know it must have been a traumatic time for you all, especially with the enquiry and Caroline dying in such a tragic accident so far away.

I often recall the times in Chestnut Avenue with you and your family; also with people of our own age: Gillian Flint next door to you, Norman Evans and Derek Hancock up the road, Sheila Bailey, Betty Partridge and many others from the 40's & 50's.

Alan I know words can't express the loss you all must feel, but I hope with time there will be healing for all.

Yours sincerely in Christ.

Nigel.   The Revd. Nigel E H Newton

From Newcastle Staffordshire

Dearest Alan

We were very sad to hear about your tragic loss of Caroline.

You have been in our thoughts constantly and we want you to know we care deeply.

Please convey our deepest sympathy to Richard

Yours sincerely

Ione & Enos.

(Enos was a college friend from the early 60's)

From Stoke on Trent

Dear Alan,

We were devastated to learn about the tragedy involving your daughter.

We lost our elder daughter some years ago but due to illness and hence expected. It follows our grief was insignificant compared with the anguish you must feel at this time.

If it is any consolation time does seem to help to understand the catastrophes which occur in our lives. We hope that somehow you and your family will get relief from the memory of your wonderful daughter. Our

prayers are with you.
J A Gillamore (Mabel)

[Ex. Crewe Technical College now South Cheshire college]
    (A colleague of the late 60's)

From America
Hello Alan,
I did not anticipate writing to you under these circumstances. My brother Mark called and gave me the horrendous news.
I am deeply saddened, I hope it will give you strength to know I am sending peace, serenity and healing to you.
If I can be of any help feel free to call me, I work nights, so I am at home in the day usually by 11am. our time 7pm. Yours.
Most sincerely Andria Payne.

(A very dear friend from the 70's in California)

From Worcestershire
Dear Alan, Marjorie and Richard
You may not remember us but we met you down at The Cross House, Padstow Cornwall, back in October 1979. We brought one of your pictures and you signed it for us on the back.
When we heard the news report and heard the name Stuttle and York, we were praying it was not you, but reading the newspapers realised it as.
We just wanted to send our most deepest sympathies to you all, and your family and friends at this very sad time.
Our thoughts and prayers are with you all.
With love Anne, Nigel, Emma & Claire Stickley.

* Coming more up to date the letter we received from the Mayor of Bundaberg
Cr. Kay McDuff
12th April 2002

Dear Mr & Mrs Stuttle, family and friends
I wish to convey my deepest sympathy to you all on behalf of myself and the citizens of Bundaberg. You are foremost in our thoughts at this sad time.
The city is in shock at the news of Caroline's death in such unexpected

circumstances, as we all believed Bundaberg to be a very safe place. Thousands of visitors from all over the world visit our city regularly and have found the environment a warm and friendly one.

Right now, our competent police service have directed all their energies to finding the perpetrators to bring them to justice, and 35 members of the State Emergency Service, under the auspices of the Bundaberg City Council, have done a sterling job in assisting the police with ancillary tasks, non stop for 15 hours.

As a mother and a grandmother, I am afraid words fail me to adequately express my sympathy to you and your family at this very difficult and emotionally draining time.

Yours in thought
Kay McDuff.

Message sent 22nd April 2002

Caroline's death caused our community much grief and in her memory prayers were offered at a large community gathering in our civic theatre. Following this I laid a sheaf of predominantly blue and yellow flowers, with the touching message from Caroline's parents attached to it, under our Burnett Traffic Bridge at the site where many local citizens had placed a small white cross, a condolence book and numerous bunches of flowers.

In addition backpackers from the many Bundaberg hostels joined with me last Friday and planted a tree in our city's Botanical Gardens. At the base of this tree a plaque will bear this message.

"TROPICAL BIRCH TREE
PLANTED IN MEMORY OF
CAROLINE ANN STUTTLE
BACKPACKER FROM YORK
BY FELLOW BACKPACKERS AND
BUNDABERG CITY MAYOR CR KAY MCDUFF
19 APRIL 2002"

While not everyone got to meet Caroline during her short time with us in the City, I can assure you she will be lovingly remembered by it's citizens.
Cr. Kay McDuff.

A card with a message from a child in Bundaberg left at the memorial site

Dear family
I am only seven years old and my name is Janessa and my sister is six we

would love to say to Caroline how sorry we are that anybody would do this.

Accompanying these delightful words from a child was a drawing of Caroline.

A postcard of Banff national park Alberta, Canada and placed in an envelope at the site...

To Caroline with love
In deepest sympathy for you and all your loved ones, wishing you could be travelling still, having happy travels and visiting beautiful Alberta and all of Australia.
May the angels take you into heaven and rest peacefully in your new home.
From Jaime, Calgary, Canada

It appeared that the whole world was grieving with us, a card was sent from Australia addressed Mr & Mrs Stuttle Caroline's parents (the girl who died in Bundaberg) York, England. We received it thanks to our Royal Mail service.
The card was with the verse, as many now will be familiar, Don't stand at my grave and weep. Also a letter included.
I was reading this article in the Sunday mail and cried for your family as my sister in Holland lost her son and could not get over his death (brain tumour) I sent her the same card as I send you. It helped her a great deal, and I hope it will do the same for you. I hope it will find your place as I don't know your address
With all my love Maria Vandarhaar.

Back in Bundaberg and another message left at the site
Dear Caroline
I'm sorry you had to leave so young and so far away from home. Your family must feel hopeless. When I found out that a young girl was killed I started to cry. I am 12 years old and care so much about you but, I know you have gone to heaven.
From Talisa

At the end of this message is a picture of child's hands holding daffodils.

All these expressions of personal emotion are quite staggering and It makes me so proud to have had a daughter that so many people are taking the trouble to express their grief quite openly.

From Dubai
Dear Mr Stuttle,
I am simply writing to express my feelings of sympathy and admiration, having read your warm and dignified words of advice to other parents. I have two daughters who I am away from for long periods of time. You are an inspiration to those who have not even had their lives impacted by such sadness as you have had to face.
I saw your words on the BBC news web-site and was compelled to write.
Your sincerely Michael Guy.

On a postcard from France
Dear Mr & Mrs Stuttle,
Thank you so much for your brave message to parents. I let my children go travelling and mercifully, they returned. However life is such a risky business, whether we live it to the full or not, the risks won't go away. To write such words now is both courageous and generous towards all the young people who need to go out and experience the world.
I cannot tell you how sorry I am that Caroline is not with you now.
Very best wishes, Jill Shepherd – a Parent.

A family sending a brave message
To Alan, Marjorie and Richard,
We are so sorry.
Our daughter, Shirine (30) was murdered in China in May 2000
Sheila, Clive, Liame & Kiera

From York
Dear Alan, this is a tiny card, but it comes with a wealth of feeling for yourself and family. I was so shocked when I heard. Having three children who had taken gap years to travel, my overriding thought was why Caroline? I went to York Minster and lit a candle for her trying to connect with events.
I do hope that when you travel to unite with the actual place, your path may be eased. Sincerely Audrey Greaves
You probably don't remember me I met you on a painting course at the Tec. And subsequently you gave us space in your studio when I was

running Micklegate Artists. For which many thanks.
All good wishes for your transfer to the Scarborough studio.
Yours Audrey.

Simple words that bring it home.

From friends in Birmingham
Lynne and Phil make their own greetings cards on their computer.
Thinking of you
At times like this we can't help remembering how fragile life is.
      Inside
May you find strength in the love of family
And the warm embrace of friends
Our thoughts are with you
Love from Lynne and Phil XXX

These words meant a lot and really hit home

From another friend in North Yorkshire
Dear Alan,
I have, like so many others, been terribly upset about this awful tragedy, and my thoughts have been with you. Now as you embark on this pilgrimage I send you both my love and deepest sympathy. I also wish for you strength and peace be with you.
Richard Whitley

The trip to Australia was gruelling but made easier by the well organised BBC. Journalist and very sympathetic camera man. For a week we were thrown together on a whirlwind of interviews press conferences and the like, there were times when we actually laughed. The team was completed by the addition of the photographer from Sydney. We all said we could not of wished for a nicer more professional hard working team to help us through.

On our last day in Sydney we were given a card as we left, again the words were written,
Don't stand at my grave and weep lovingly penned by the giver.
The words that touched us the most were,
For a journalist the definition of news is, ordinary people in extraordinary circumstances.

To Alan, Richard and Jan
Three of the most extraordinary people I have ever met.
I will never forget our time together, thank you for enriching our lives,
and to Caroline, for that is her legacy.
From Christa and Keith with love.
The picture on the front of the card was by Pablo Picasso two crossed
hands.
That wonderful team had most certainly held our hand and led us
through some of our darkest moments. Just as I had taken Caroline's
hand as we walked together through her childhood.

My thanks once again for all the wonderful work done by Christa, Keith
and Nigel.

Chapter Eight

We all tend to think our children are wonderful and do only want to remember the good times and the joy they bring, feeling proud of their achievements, but when you hear a tribute from a college tutor who probably has spent more time with them in their final years, it really did fill me with pride to hear this **tribute read by the tutor at Caroline's funeral.**

23rd April 2002

I am privileged to have been asked to speak today about Caroline and honoured to share my thoughts on why she was so loved and so special to us all.

Caroline had one of those rare personalities which makes it impossible to think of her without feeling glad, or to smile because you knew her. She possessed a great many characteristics which drew people close to her.

On first meeting Caroline, it was striking how kind, confident and intuitive she was. You remember her afterwards, not because she shouted the loudest or craved the most attention, but because she glowed with warmth, intelligence and compassion.

Everyone who met Caroline loved her wonderful spirit. Her sense of humour, in particular, was bright, sweet natured, and on one occasion a little daring, which showed us that she was also independent and self-reliant. She responded to humour well, and was easy to make laugh, something I know we all enjoyed doing because to see Caroline smile made us smile too.

Caroline was incredibly friendly and continually surrounded by others. It was a rare sight to see Caroline by herself. Her family and her friends were terribly important to her, and so many of her every day concerns and future dreams involved them all. She was a quintessential young woman, so deservedly popular, so sociable, so energetic and so animated. A friend once commented that it was if she ran on Duracell batteries, because her energy never ran out. Many will remember her insatiable conversation and talkative nature. Caroline always fitted so much into her life.

Caroline was an especially loving person. She had a great capacity for kindness and consideration for others. She expressed emotion easily, and was a very tactile person, she gave frequent hugs of friendship, sympathy or tenderness. She loved, and was loved by, her family, her boyfriend and a great number of close friends. She had too, a terrific love of animals, I remember how attached she was to her family's pets.

These would have been reason enough to want to be part of Caroline's life, but other more consummate qualities made her the person we all knew. In Caroline, the qualities that made her sociable and popular were enhanced by more giving attributes. Caroline had a wonderfully generous spirit; she was such a giving person. Regardless of what she was doing, she would unthinkingly put it to one side so she could help others, or simply be there for them. Caroline combined studying hard with working to save for her dream; her family with her active social life that she shared with so many friends. Caroline would always find time to help others, sending thoughtful messages, sharing class notes, listening to others problems, giving lifts in her car. She would put aside her saving so that she could send cards and mementoes to show she cared.
Again, Caroline unselfishly thought of others all the time. Caroline's family were important to her, and she had many close friends, but she shared her energy equally among them all.

Caroline was naturally sensitive and supportive of other people. She genuinely wanted those around her to be happy and if they were not, neither was she. Caroline was delighted by the success of others and never felt any envy or jealousy about their accomplishments. Caroline encouraged others to do well. She knew intuitively how to help those around her, giving practical support when needed. For example, lending her revision notes to classmates, or arranging accommodation for a friends arrival in Australia. She would do anything to help the people she knew. But it was the emotional support she gave that helped others the most. Caroline was truly able to empathise and understand the feelings of others in order to know how to help them the best. She would always give advise and reassurance no matter what time of day or night. Caroline would put her own worries aside and focus on the problems of those around her. The people she helped were taken seriously, were not judged, and the advice she gave was wise and from the heart.

Caroline was clearly a mature, patient and determined young woman, which is perhaps why she was also such an outstanding student, whom I am deeply honoured to have taught. She adored Psychology right from the start, and her talent was immediately obvious. I believe Caroline was attracted to psychology because the subject aims to understand and help others, as she herself endeavoured to do. She enjoyed the analytical side of the course and flourished when writing her own research, which she threw herself into with dedication and enthusiasm. In fact she worked so hard, we nicknamed her "Caroline Study" after she wrote her name this way on an exam paper. The resolute side of Caroline's personality drove her through her studies- her determination and ambition to achieve her goals never faltered.

Early on in her studies, Caroline set herself some tough targets, which required such hard work many would have been discouraged from attempting them, but Caroline was well on the way to making them become a reality. She worked hard to save for her travels while studying furiously to obtain the grades needed to read psychology at Manchester University. And of course she got them. I was thrilled, but not remotely surprised when I saw her exam results.

Caroline had her heart set on her career in forensic psychology, an arduous career and by no means an easy choice. Yet if we think about what we know about this amazing young woman, then it is obvious she would have succeeded. Caroline possessed all the right qualities: she was sensitive, compassionate and non-judgemental so could understand those that needed help. And she had the rational and resilient side needed to work in a challenging and consuming career. I know Caroline would have achieved anything she put her mind to.

Caroline's wonderful qualities must not end here. Her dreams must be kept alive and others encouraged to follow them. She was too precious for us to just stop now, and to say, "she would have been". We must learn from Caroline and inspire the same kindness, compassion and generosity in others. We must remind ourselves not to waste a single moment, to set goals and to achieve them, just like Caroline did. We must not let Caroline's glow fade away.

Chapter Nine

The New Zealand Experience
16th February 2004

It has always amazed me how quickly you can travel in comfort and relative ease around our world. In a few short hours we find ourselves in a completely different environment.

Remembering and looking back at your past life in a selection of pictures and memories, how quickly we can travel in the mind, from one part of our life to another. Some sad and others full of joy, yet seldom in the future, which is perhaps just as well for most of us. We would not wish to go there at some times in our life.

When we all pass into that dominion called death, or is it everlasting life? In a world that is so near to ours only a different vibration, we all I am sure reflect on what we have experienced in our life. We have that precious thing called experience without it how can we grow or pass on knowledge. If not to other people then perhaps we can ourselves learn. Perhaps these experiences help us in our future actions. Who can really predict a future life?

I start this journey taking parts of the past with me, always in my heart that can never change, nor would I wish them to. I look forward with a great feeling of positive energy propelling me forward into my future times such as they will be. Often I feel a great coldness in my heart from the wound that will never heal, for part of me died with my child on that doleful and evil day of her murder.

This journey to Australia and onward to New Zealand was not as traumatic as the last one. I went on to New Zealand, perhaps to make a new start, certainly so with my painting and art. It has to date inspired me in a different way.

I am using the past to forge a future, using loss and despair to make s omething good. Looking at things anew, perhaps through the eyes of the young, because I often feel the presence, perhaps of my daughter and good can surely be born of evil.

19th February 2004

Arrived in New Zealand and made a start painting watercolours. It was very pleasant working outside in such summer weather in February.

My first impression was of how very much like England everything is only on a larger scale, the greens are so rich, weather conditions change very fast, rain, wind, then in a short time later, sunshine, so much like my beloved Yorkshire.

As I painted the tumbling waters at a place called Meeting of the Waters, where two rivers meet, I felt the peace enter into me, a sought of healing, mentally and spiritually. Very slowly I felt relaxation, this really is a beautiful country to relax in.

It is always an adventure to visit a different country or area, but this was an almost out of this world experience. Perhaps a feeling of coming home of finding somewhere where, perhaps, for the first time in my life I could make a home as I want it to be, space, fresh air, greens of so much vibration and lush large leaves, that the imagination could run wild, time for freedom to express something completely different, a different aspect of myself and what I have worked with these past years.

We must never hold onto the past, it is a forgotten land where only memories hold sway. Some bringing regret, some bringing comfort. We may need some security in our lives but then, what is security when life can be ended so quickly, youth is no deterrent to ending of life (we read about it every day).

When you have been driven through great sorrow as I have been in the past years, death, divorce, deception, lies, wicked malicious jealousies and theft. The ending of my gallery that I have owned for over thirty years, the selling of a family home, the loss of a daughter, what more can I endure. These negative energies would destroy any human being, this is where there is a great need for change and a moving forward to things new, people to meet and places to go. One thing that I hold dear to myself is one's talent, ability and positive energy, this can never be destroyed by others, only by yourself.

To let go of the past there is often a need to burn bridges, to let go, this is not the easiest thing to do, sometimes I think it may have been the wrong thing to do. I am sure that the past must be put out of the way, never forgotten but in it's correct place. Remembering the good times, the happy times and there have been many.

During this short visit to New Zealand I have had deep thoughts of what I have left behind in U.K. my home for many years. The dearest thing I, at present own, is my daughters grave, that is all I hold dear, the rest is air and dust, she will be there for eternity.

In New Zealand I feel I have found a challenge, the colours and the light lifts me and that is so very much needed in a situation like this. As I work with my art and spirituality I find the colours healing and gently calming, I just go with it, the colours are a delight to the painters eye, a new world. I have travelled Italy, Spain, Switzerland, Germany, Austria, Australia, Canada, America and have found beauty in all countries so nothing more can be expected or said, that is for future times and future dates, the challenge will be there.

We make plans to do things in our retirement, next year, next week, but life gets in the way always. Never make plans too far ahead, do it now, go for your dreams and ideas they may never come again. How many poems have died with the morning light? How many people with dreams have died?

I thank the people who helped me through this time and my remaining family, most people were very supportive, some didn't know what to say, some turned their back completely, some stabbed me in the back, but strangely, the ones you would not expect to do so, were of the most help, almost strangers. Some so called friends hurt me deeply.

I did not expect that at the tender age of sixty four to be going on another adventure, perhaps to be the most exciting of my life, certainly with the most freedom that I have ever had, in every way. The adventure itself will be part of the healing of the spirit and the heart. The spirit being always eternal and the body will fall to dust. What we do will surely go on forever.

We go through out lives saying "if only I had done this or that" always questioning and regretting things that we can now never change. It is the true measure of a man to make the best use of the talents God has given him, therein, always is his strength of future times. Never to be afraid to change and change again, it has always been the nature of man to do so, nature must sometimes be heard in the heart, as well as with common sense. The shedding of an old skin and emerging the other side, hopefully more positive and wise. Call it the death of an old life into a new challenge and opportunities. Perhaps the footsteps of my child has opened up my mind to new challenges and perhaps once again I may see angels in my life.

During our trip the weather has been the worst for one hundred and fifty years. Rain, wind, flooding, "and this is summer".

On arriving in Auckland we stepped outside the airport and met a demonstration of howling wind, rain and sun all in the matter of fifteen minutes "Oh well". I must admit it was rather disappointing to say the least, but being half way around the world you can't pack your bags and go home. So on we went, week one, week two, not much change but then the sun came out and all seemed to change, perhaps it was a symbol of good and bad, black and white, that which is in all our lives.

The weather was now almost perfect for painting watercolours which was, of course, one of the reasons I came to New Zealand. The landscapes were a complete revelation to me, such diversity and beauty. This day I painted Mount Taranaki from the lake, great day, such a feeling of positive energy and warmth, things were getting better in all ways.

Yet another perfect day and I painted in the beautiful park, a little paradise. Yes, I was feeling like my new positive self again.

1st March

My son Richard came over from Australia for a week or more, it was so good to see him. My little boy is now a handsome young man of twenty six. I was delighted he was doing some painting also. We spent a few days together just painting the sea, lakes, trees, mountain etcetera. Richard produced some very good work, and what is more important, has lots of enthusiasm, not only for painting but has a didgeridoo and can even play it, he loves his skateboarding activities. A very positive way of going forward into his future, which up to date has not been that easy.

Weather has now improved even more sunshine. Painting in the park finishing off previously started paintings, Richard joined me, a very pleasant day.

A bright but very windy day, a feeling of change in the air, the onset of an autumn feel. Funny to think we will be going back to UK. to the start of our spring "I hope".

I listened to an old broadcast tape I made with the BBC. Woman's Hour, it seems so long ago now and I sound a different person even in the voice.

Richard went to the skateboard park and we painted on the beach in New Plymouth. A good day and good fun.

We went to the glow-worm caves. It was a long way but Jan drove us there safely, that was a new experience for us all.

Another day, another painting. Richard and I started a painting of the lighthouse at Egmont again with Mount Taranaki in the background. What great space and freedom.

5th March

Painted at Lake Mangamahoe with Richard, very warm and pleasant, I used my camcorder to record the progress of our paintings.

As time rolled by, far too fast, I produced a selection of some ten or so pictures in watercolours and I like to display some of my paintings in different countries. Jan & I were staying at a beautiful little house near a river, the area called Meeting of the Waters, a great place for a small showing. I decided to place a small advertisement in the local press, that I was over from the UK. painting watercolours of the area. The press were interested in the paintings I had done for Granada TV's Coronation Street, so they also gave me a free write up, which of course was so nice. Setting out my intentions and ideas for what I hoped is to be my future. New Plymouth is full of devoted fans of Corri, I did the paintings some years ago. It was so nice also to move on from the public interest in my daughter's death in Australia. Again a moving on and moving forward. The little exhibition was a great success around two hundred people turned out for my watercolour demonstration, we were all delighted, and as I hope to return to New Plymouth for a longer time next year, we hope to do it again "we will do it again".

19th March
Richard leaves us for Rotorua to meet up with friends who are doing a tour of New Zealand. It is always so sad to see your children go to do something else "there is always next time".
It has been a good productive week with Richard and I, we could not have done it without Janet and her always caring and outstanding help.
When will I see my little boy again? Well! I think about him often as I do Caroline. I will always have their company in my heart.
The pain of loss will never leave Richard and me, it is something we will always live with, we can sometimes move on with our lives into a stage we may call happiness.
The birds are singing in my garden and we all go on to a new adventure, yet I still think, where will I be tomorrow.
It is so good to see Richard go on his adventures, the sun is shining but there is still a coldness in my heart which will never leave.

The day has come and we must say goodbye to New Zealand the end of our wonderful trip, to see Janet's family and we have met what I hope will become new friends. One wonderful meeting was made at the exhibition by a very old and close friend whom I have known for many years in York who now lives in New Zealand where he moved in his retirement some two years ago, his daughter saw the press advertisement and called him to come over to join us for a few hours "the world seems so small sometimes"
Janet and I went to so many places and met so many people, We really did have a wonderful time. We went out to dinners, barbeques and drinks, it was a lot of fun, as well as that which I had to do for myself.

Did it do what I expected it to? Yes and so very much more. It gave us a future to ponder over, my dream is to have a studio in UK. and possibly now one in New Zealand "Is it just a dream or will it become reality in the not too distant future".
It brought healing with my painting, with ideas of working in a different place and if I am spared to live to a ripe old age, I hope to fill some of my dreams with that reality.
Even though my family have had to bear such a terrible loss I have always had the solace of my talent and art to push me onwards, no one can take

away your abilities and self respect. Trust in yourself, go onwards and make changes in life which you may never have dreamed of. Age is of no importance, great loss needs a great change, it is no use sitting with your head in the air saying "why me" It has been and you have to get on with it. Disasters of this nature affect people in different ways, it is the healthy way to move forwards, with perhaps a new freedom. What would that lost loved one want you to do? Sit and wallow in self pity and regret the things that should have been done and now can never be?

I am carrying on with my creative powers, setting up a little painting prize for the school which Richard and Caroline attended in Huntington near York, to help youngsters, as I have said all along, to follow their dreams and what is more, their hearts. If a student uses their talent for art well then they need every encouragement.

Many will, and I say this with a heavy heart, taste the same as we have done in future times. Don't be defeated, use their love and spirit to move forward on the winds of time, and until we all meet again in that yet to be explored world beyond ours, use your time well, least time, in it's unyielding arms, uses you. It is always better to save a life than waste it "I have done this".

During many years of using my creative abilities I have been so blessed with the healing energy that the use of any creative talent can produce. I have always felt that the very physical act of putting paint on canvas or writing poetry can bring about a feeling of well being and healing.
Sometimes it can be the different ways of painting that can bring about a release of emotions, for example the use of a pallet knife to apply paint on canvas can give a sense of freedom and expression. The use of colour is so important in life whether it is through a creative art, within the environment or by the clothes we wear. Colour can cheer others along with you, it is like the saying 'smile and the world smiles with you, cry and you cry alone' we must stay strong and use whatever talent we have to lead us through the dark back into the light.

Chapter Ten

Some times are hard but life goes on, and as time passes, again the shadows hang over me. That wound in my heart, spirit and soul will never heal, it can only be lived with, every hour, day, month and as the years pass away all we are left with are memories, those of our past joys and follies of our life. If it is to be that when we leave this world we do move on into another existence of life maybe then too we will look at our past life's experiences and recall the memories shared with our loved ones, who really knows? we shall know when we take that journey.

There are times when in waking or in sleep state our mind becomes full of thoughts that make no sense, some good, some bad, some indifferent, is it maybe that at these times it is when we are being guided.

Lets not allow hate to rule our life for it will only bring hate to ourselves. A heart may be full of grief and hurt yet our hearts are also full of love, and the power of prayer can be far more powerful and will bring about healing. Remembering that nothing can destroy the love you hold if you keep positive thoughts which will in time reap positive actions and peace will resume in your life, this will in time rekindle faith in humanity.

I try to remember that we are in God's hands and that we are all part of that universal consciousness. Not a leaf falls that is not known about, so, most certainly, are our tears of both joy and sadness. I pray that this life we journey is not at our due time the end, but a new beginning roaming faraway on the river of life anew ever onwards. We can not right the wrongs that we may have done, we can learn from them, trying always to do the best we can, going forward and not looking back to what might have been.

It is my belief now that the only way to move forward in life when all only seems darkness and despair, is to carry on with as much of your everyday normal activities as you can. It will not be easy, things will never be as they were yesterday or last year.

Life is to be enjoyed, never be afraid to laugh, it is no crime, slowly life will be less painful and the joy of things and events in life will return.

I set myself tasks to do, as an artist painted in a different way in different areas, I used the sadness as an energy, a very positive energy. Be strong and the strength will be given to you. The positive power of prayer does bring comfort and can be felt in the heart and uplifts the mind. Never give in to the darker feelings, go out into the sunshine when ever possible, smell the flowers, look at the sky, know that the world, even though sometimes it feels as if you heart is broken, is a beautiful place.

As sure as night follows day your pain will ease and parts of your life will heal and change. Be positive, send out healing not hate. Though fools may laugh and break what you have made, with love here on earth within your heart, is the kingdom of heaven. Go in peace and tranquillity will follow.

The Hole of Horcum where we went flying models & walking

Chapter Eleven

Time has now passed by and I have organised a bursary for Huntington School, called The Richard and Caroline Painting Fund. It is a bursary for students interested in developing their artistic abilities. I am delighted that the first presentation has been made and a cheque for five hundred pounds has been awarded to the first student. She is going to use the money to go to New York, to create a painting for the school to record her trip and the ideas it inspired, it will provide a good record for future years. I intend the award to be presented every year for the foreseeable future. It is my way of saying thank you for all the love and kindness my family and I have been shown during the many years working and living in York, a truly wonderful City where I have painted for the past thirty years.

It is important to do something for local people and local charities, it is something we can all see and enjoy. (seems strange Caroline's first choice was to go to New York)

July 2004

It has been a long hard journey, a pathway of tears and heartfelt regrets, in many things said and done during the past two years. I have changed my life completely, not understanding, finishing my business, selling my properties in York and moving to my little gallery in Scarborough where I expect to live and work for the foreseeable future. I can walk out of my studio and be by the sea in under five minutes walk. I have painted the waves crashing and the moody skies many reflecting my own moods.

Old friends call me and come to visit. It is so good to keep in touch with people I knew in my other life. It seems so long ago now, yet really in time it is but a heartbeat.

I know now it is to see me people come, not for what they can get from me and that is the difference between real friends.

At my gallery in Scarborough was the last walk Caroline and I had together down to the South bay by the sea, I remember saying how proud I was of her and what she was doing. Funny, we also talked of what I wanted when I died as she and Richard would do it for me, little did I know, in how a short time things would change forever. It is good we do not know many things in life, that which we call future dreams can turn into nightmares.

I would like to thank all the friends, strangers and people I have met from all over the world who took the time to write to my now depleted and broken family, to say how sad they were about this terrible thing that had robbed my daughter of her life and my family of a future. A whole generation has been wiped out, her children and children's children...now never to be.

I would like to thank with all my heart my very close friends Brian and Mary, who have always been there for me. Through all the pain, all the hurt and torment given to me through, what I can only say, were wicked, thoughtless and selfish people. As the sands of time turn so will their actions be revealed and lies uncovered to the light of truth.

And finally to Janet, who has always been there for me, Caroline met her on her last visit to Scarborough. Janet has given me unconditional support in all my undertakings and I know, has been my tower of strength and comfort even in my darkest hour. What can I say about such a person who gives pure love and shows it in every way.
I have only known Janet for a short time but in my hour of deepest need she was there, when to the shame of others, who I have known for thirty or more years, were nowhere to be seen, I am not really bothered now it all seems immaterial now, bitterness will only hurt me and of that I have had enough...

There are many who say that there is no such things as pre-planned events in our destiny. I met Janet in August 2000, at that time I was travelling around, working a lot in this country and abroad. Janet's life was filled with her own work but found time for meditation, during one such time she was impressed to write some words. I have seen the paper which she dated as always...

26.9.00
As I search deep within I find peace, there lies an answer to all the questions, I am listening for a note that I may recognise. Is there a piece of music playing somewhere for me? How can I hear words when I listen to music? Easy - let your soul feel the words, let your heart express it's joy as it enters into an unknown realm of possibilities. Open heart, open mind, opens doors, keys are offered, advise offered, love offered, do not miss any opportunity that comes your way. You, as a child of the universe, must be open to all possibilities come out of the mists of time, grieving child weep no more, allow joy into your world once more.

These words not only echo my thoughts but offer me hope and comfort for the future.
Do we call these meaningful coincidences or serendipity or was she an angel of mercy being prepared for the events to come?

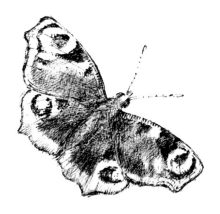

I shall turn my eyes to the Bridge of life, shoulder my heavy
burden and walk with pride onwards through this time we call
life until I too shall return to the world of pure light, love and
spirit where all truth and goodness rule forever

Chapter Twelve

The final journey

23rd September 2004

The final chapter to this ordeal, this journey most unexpected, certainly unwanted, to be lived through, felt, laughed and cried through.

The thought of going to Australia again to relieve the agony of mind, spirit and very being, it is a cup that I would not want to drink of. To see the alleged murderer of my child face to face. What will I think, do or feel? Something or nothing? The certain ruin of my life as I knew it, so secure, so certain in it's future of going on in the same old way I had for some thirty years of constancy and doing the same things, certain in the future of grandchildren and a happy life, to be so changed in so many disastrous ways, never imagined or dreamed of in my worst nightmare, so much of it brought about by spite greed and perhaps envy of other people's myths and fertile imaginations.

This time is difficult, reliving all that has passed, not only the death of my daughter, but the positive thoughts of making something positive out of this and many other disasters that have happened in the passed seven years, wrong ways to go and right ways to go, our only richness is hindsight.

As we look at ourselves in the past and future times, for surely there will be a future even in death, for I truly believe that our spirit lives on. Perhaps we are inspired by the world of spirit in our everyday tasks, certainly all great works by mortal men is inspired, we are given strength to go onward and fulfil our allotted tasks. While we still have light, before we ourselves are received into the cold bosom of the earth as surely one day we must, our hearts hands and eyes will no longer be, yet our spirit will survive.

During the next few weeks Caroline's remaining family and I will be photographed, interviewed, recorded for TV. all around the world, simply because our daughter, Caroline, the name chosen has been so cruelly taken from us in a land so far away from our gentle and beautiful England. A land so spectacular in it's grandeur and vast expanses was where Caroline was to end her days, a land that my daughter was so enthralled with.

The days pass yet no end to the pain. I try to work but can never really clear my mind and heart of what has happened, I have not been instructed in how to deal with this turmoil of soul. I write down these pages in the hope that through reading them I may perhaps understand what is going on, a feeling of unreality sometimes touches me, I live in the past for comfort, for the memories I shall always have, no power on earth can take that from me. I go to my garden when I need to, but now it is the garden of my mind. Remembering the warm summers, the winter snow and special Christmas times. Oh, my God, why has this been given to me? Then I say why not. I am no different than anyone else. The plans we make in life are always going to be changed by nature, for all men rise and fall.

To do ones best, to strive for perfection, to push onward through the turmoil of ever changing life's rivers and boulders is all we can expect of ourselves, when we fall we should do it bravely and never flinch, try to hold back the tears, which what ever we do will surely come, as winter shall give way to spring onwards and perhaps upwards is the ultimate aim and goal. Push forward though your heart is broken and you feel you've had enough, perhaps of life itself...

These are the thoughts that pass through the mind of someone who is grieving for a loved one. As I have been writing this I am very much aware of someone near me, perhaps to give me the comfort and confidence to face what surely I have to, just a gentle love is all that I feel. I would encourage those that have been bereaved to sit and write their feelings down and perhaps some comfort may be given to them in a wonderful way. Help is always near us, we must simply ask and it will be given in many ways. Prayer and love will always take precedence over revenge and hatred, love is the finest power in this world and we are told the next also. It is so simple yet we find it difficult to understand in this busy bustling world, there is so much to understand, I doubt we ever will.

24th September 2004

Richard texted, he is fine now he is over the jet lag and will find his way to Bundaberg 'that dreaded name' in the next few days. A very brave young man, I am very proud of both my children. Along with the heart break I have known great joy. Perhaps all life is on a balance of scales, from the depths of despair to the heights of joy.

Christa rang from the BBC. with great news. She will be able to write the forward to my book, I am so very pleased. We are so lucky to know people like her, so feeling and dedicated to what she is doing.

Photographs for the Daily Telegraph, as always very caring and detailed work. I expect these to be the last ones on this subject. It has been so good being photographed doing my art this past month. It's good it's an end.

Real Radio rang and I gave a short interview, words, words they seem to flow though I don't think I am saying anything different than when it started. What knowledge hindsight gives...If only.

I spent most of the day painting out of the windows of my old VW. The one that Caroline and I made our trips to the Dales, Scotland and visits to the beautiful Yorkshire moors. Her seat by me so very empty now but the memories are always with me and she lives always in my heart.

As I paint the waves in Scarborough crashing against the shore it reminds me of the constant movement of our lives and passions, ever changing and ever onward, that is the way of things, change, for a still pond can be stifling when it lacks the oxygen of life.

"I am so pleased I am an unknown artist, it can be very hard work, these interviews"

Saturday the time passes, this time next week I shall have started out on my long journey to Australia and it brings me to wonder, when on that fateful day my daughter started out on her journey that was to end so tragically in that faraway land, what was in her mind? Was she excited? of course she was looking forward to the adventure of a lifetime, which in her case it was. I told her it would be the time of her life, and so it was... the end of her life.

Today as I looked round this beautiful world of the sea and sky, what would I do differently if this was to be my last day on earth? simple things, what would I eat, do, say, experience. In some strange way I treat my days in a more respectful way, I use my time and don't let time use me. I fill my days with doing things that are dear to my heart, smell the air, hear the song of the birds and the crashing of the waters on the shore near my home in Scarborough. It is very clear to me that nothing lasts forever, not even us our homes or our relationships. Perhaps we have to experience all, before understanding the whole.

The thought of death, an end to us is so incomprehensible, it can never be imagined yet in a few short moments it could end and will at some time for us all. Death is no respecter of age, time or place we will all tread that pathway in some future time, perhaps tomorrow. We must all try to use the now and enjoy the moment for that is all we have in the nature of things.

Sunday 26th September 2004

Today I shall enjoy the whole of my day by remembering and thinking that this time next week we will be flying to Australia a thing I don't want to do and would never have wished to in this awful time. Not that Australia is not a beautiful country, nothing to do with that.

This morning I went to the Yorkshire moors where we had travelled and walked and played with the children over many years, perhaps it will be the last time I see it who knows, It is truly beautiful. On to Pickering Castle where we took the children from school, so very long ago. I walked around this 1000 year old building thinking of what it had seen over the centuries. As I walked into the keep of this historic place I received a telephone call from Australia, it was the Guardian newspaper reporter, when you think, it must be a first, what progress we have made and yet how fragile life is now as it was 1000 years ago, times change but not our pain. Our hearts feel now as then, there would be pain and love for our children, it was always so and the day passes and autumn shows it's colours to the trees and the landscape we pass through. We called at the honey farm where, in the heady days of summer, the bees are so active, producing the life-giving honey, working together as one unit, not killing the other without reason. We could learn a lot from the natural things around us, but while we kill each other for money or religious beliefs there will never be any hope for humanity. It has been said that perhaps we can not do great things but we can do small things with great love.

I shall go to Australia and paint through my daughters eyes, the tree of life and shall enclose a copy in my forthcoming writings that it may send the thought of a young girl's love of life around our world and hope it may bring, if not peace, then the thought of what we are doing to each other in this our ever restless and self destructive world. Perhaps we can start with a small thing that we can do, we can, with great love, as love is the greatest power that we can feel, with this, nothing can hurt us and use the shield of truth. The pen is truly mightier than any sword, the truth will always be written at some future time.

Monday
Today I went to York. I drove along the gentle highways changing in colour with the scenes of autumn. I visited Caroline's grave, the stone with Caroline Ann Stuttle has little changed, the flowers from her birthday have now died, I take them away. I wish I could once again take my laughing smiling child away. I sprinkle the autumn leaves of many

colours on her grave. This time and time's are enough to break my heart, perhaps now we must begin to say goodbye, her spirit must now be long away from this little grave this resting place of so many dreams, hopes and fears.

What sort of world have we! to pass to our children, when only death is present.

The trial in Australia has now started, I wish they could feel the desolation and emptiness of a parent's broken heart. God takes her to him but leaves me my dreams as they help to ease this bleeding heart.

I drive past many familiar places I have known for the past thirty years or more but in some strange way they have changed. It is like looking into a mirror and not recognising yourself perhaps time has left me by. Perhaps it was my time to move onward and forwards into future times.

I painted in York today, something I always like to do, so many people I know came and said hello and shook my hand, so warm and caring, all will be thinking of my little family at this sad time.

I try to think of the past for comfort, it's a way of finding a form of solace. I pass my old gallery now changed completely, If only walls could speak of the last six hundred years in Micklegate York... if only... Christmas, springs, summers and autumns that I knew so well have passed into history, perhaps in some future times I will visit my studio in York.

The evening was spent enjoyably visiting my lodge in York a great comfort knowing that I have so much support throughout the world - my family and I.

28th September 2004

A busy day but rather tired, the news keeps coming through about Caroline on the TV. and radio, scenes like a story that I am not part of somewhat unreal, perhaps I shall wake up and will find it all a dream. The details are horrific things I don't really want to know and yet have to know how our child met her death. It is important to me, one thing I know is that she put up a fight to stop this revolting man but all in vain. My mind goes to the fall from the bridge in the darkness, falling, falling and then the sickening sound of hitting the dried out riverbed, the splitting of bones, the bursting of the skull and ripping of blood vessels, then the sound of silence and darkness, one moment terrified by a thing, a poor excuse for a human being. What a brutal end seeing that face and smelling his stench near you and fighting for your life in this darkest of places. The stillness after the fall, the last desperate breath, the dimming eyes as she tried to cling onto life. What must have gone on in that split second of conscious mind and dying body! Mum, Dad, Richard, home, the green of England. The screams everyone heard were not of this world, she was terrified out of her wits, the fall must have taken her out of this world so quickly, I know an angel would have taken her gently to Jesus the saviour of children. Now no one will ever hurt her again and she will be forever young.

News and the details are always on the TV. and Richard is doing a wonderful job, if you can call it that. I have two wonderful children, don't I?, for both have touched the hearts of the world. What a lucky man I am to have this most wonderful gift. I am so proud.

Gave another interview with a very nice lady for the national press with some photographs also, sometimes it helps to talk about what is going on in your mind.

I was talking about the Richard and Caroline Painting Bursary for Huntington School and how we should give our young people both advice and money. I give £500 to the winner of the bursary each year to allow them to go and paint where they will. As a result of the interview there has been a donation of £1,000 for my painting bursary, you see how good people can be and it will give some young person the chance in life to do something they want to help them achieve their aim or goal.

Richard texted all is ok. We are in touch most days. A few days and I will be in Oz.

Along with Ian, Caroline's boyfriend and her friend, Sarah, her travelling companion who has been so brave throughout this time. I do hope they have a wonderful future I am quite sure they will.

Today I managed to paint for a few hours, my solace has always given me healing and it's most important to continue. It is most important to keep as fit and active as you can. I walk and run up stairs. Today I had my blood pressure checked A1. I shall need it for what is yet to come.

29th September 2004

A good day weather wise, worked outside. Richard rang from Oz to fill me in on what is going on at the trial, all the details of what happened to Caz very upsetting, it always brings it back to you.

I told Richard of my idea of painting a tree for Caroline, Richard can do one and I will do one for my book.

Interview with Calendar TV., it went ok. but very draining.

Our friend Wendy came over to see us for a hug, always good to see her but sad, she too needs to share what happened to her.

Getting ready for Australia.

30th September 2004

The day we make our start for Oz. The important thing is to keep going as a normal day. I finished a fun commission and delivered it, also got paid for it! Money for expenses, because even though times are sad, you still have to earn a living. I always have to date, and always will... who knows, perhaps the best is not passed as many have said, I feel it's yet to come...

3rd October 2004

The start of this awful trip to Australia, all went well to start with, taxi arrived on time and everything seems to be going quite well, this is the journey I would not wish to do.

The Daily Mail article went quite well I thought, It was mostly mine, funny to see Caroline's picture and my name, it's so long ago and yet you can touch the moment.

I am writing this passage while in the air (in an aircraft of course) bumpy and late taking off but it beats walking or sailing!

I feel, in a way, very angry, sad and rather empty as I have said many times, on this journey should not have been.

The hope that it will be all concluded in this next few weeks is very gratifying, then perhaps, God willing, I can make a start with the rest of my time on this beautiful planet and it is very beautiful, you know, there are good and bad in every nation and creed, the problem is, what is meant by good or bad?

It's a funny thing flying this way again, the way Caroline went two years ago, the time has seemed to pass quickly but the pain never goes, it is always with you but sometimes joy returns for a short while. Be sure the sun will shine again for you, one of my ways of dealing with it is to think of little ways I would like to spend my time, holidays, trips to the Dales, subjects to paint, all things to look forward to. The times I spend in the past are getting fewer now. I am thinking about my teaching at the Stansted college, my new home in New Zealand or Yorkshire or wherever they are now, my dreams. Seeing my son develop his life skills and hopefully a long and fruitful life for him in future years, for life is a never ending circle of hopes and dreams deaths and rebirths always forward on a pathway that was destined before we were even born. The certain knowledge of death should not be always in the mind, for if it is, so we forget to live.

Every day in this past week this trial in Australia has been going on. The details keep coming out and this has been most distressing, I quote as it came to me. Recorded in the prison cell, spoken by the accused, laughing drifter admitted to killing the backpacker girl (this, of course, was my daughter, Caroline) no one else was heard laughing.

Ian Douglas Previte, aged 32, tells how the teenager died because she refused to let go of her handbag..... "can anyone imagine that, murdered because you refuse to give what you have worked for away.... To a drug addict... what would anyone do, would you or I give it away to a thug that was out of his skull? The thing was asked "Did Caroline put up a fight?". It replied "A BIT ..YEAH, they just don't want to fucking give them up, she didn't, it was either me or her" It goes on to say "Is no point in getting stressed about what happened, you've got to laugh", it goes on "and I've stabbed a few. Laughing, he describes killing Caroline. About the mobile phone he said "I kept it for a while, walking around with it in me pocket, I smashed it, I was going to throw it in the river." Someone else disposed of Caroline's shoulder bag, and there, I think, you have the truth of the matter, that is how much a child's life is worth. Parents be sure you are aware of all these pettifogging thieves and addicts we have about us and be sure they are waiting and watching for a chance to destroy anyone's life as it has surely mine. So if your child, friend or dear one is to take off and take their chances be sure they always go together everywhere. It is seldom two people are attacked, most of these crimes are done by cowards and will only attack young girls or boys on their own or the elderly in lonely isolated places. I don't say don't go, it's the old saying be prepared and stop it happening again to you and yours, it's up to you. Don't let a few scum spoil it for you and your dreams, I say go for it.

I had three people in my life that spoiled it for me, but they say you reap what you sow and time will tell who was right or wrong.

In a lesser degree on my return from New Zealand, after a month away, having a new floor and carpet fitted in my little gallery in Scarborough, on the day before opening some youth, along with an accomplice, kicked in my glass door, we know who it was but it is so much trouble proving it, witnesses and court, it's hardly worth it. We have had car windows smashed, windscreen wipers ripped off and wing mirrors kicked off, for what reason? for a laugh. It seems to me. The murderer of my daughter was as said by the scum bag 'you have got to laugh'.

Well I think it is time for the law abiding citizens to have their turn to laugh, don't you? I surely am and very soon. It seems that crime always wins, when people are killed for a telephone, sex, a piece of jewellery, religion or colour. This world can seem such a sad place.

It is now the second day of our journey to Australia it's a long flight but much faster than it used to be by boat. I just rest, eat and do a little writing but thinking mostly about things I could have done better and chances I have let slip by. I shall use my opportunities now and hopefully in future years. That's if I survive this trip.

The reason for this journey is simple I need to mark the bastard that killed my daughter (just for a laugh) I want to see his face just once, for it is surely not human and devoid of all feeling and morality of any kind, drugs do that to you. The people who push the muck to children are the real problem. I once read a slogan written on a wall in York, 'Feel good today - kill a pusher'. A good sentiment but we just say now 'Dob in a pusher'. It may save someone's child, brother or sister.

It is important now for all of us to go forward with our hopes and fears and let Caroline go onto her pathway as we go on ours, for it is my sure belief that we will meet again in the world of the spirit and all our sins will have to be accounted for.

What we have done with our lives will surely echo in eternity. Of the murder of a child, the bible says it's better for that man or woman that he had never been born.

If you have seen the film 'Ghost' I believe they have got it right and many near death experiences prove it, so there is no forgiving God with a long beard, we judge ourselves and evil will surely begat evil, perhaps it has already begun for some, it surely has and will very soon, we reap or harvest what we have sown.

One important thing that happens to junkies, they don't seem to live very long, they destroy their minds and their bodies. There are the exceptions, of course, they are made aware of their short comings, as do alcoholics. They can receive treatment and completely turn their lives around, and in turn, help others by going into schools and colleges, talking on the dangers of these substances. This is admirable, I have met a few who have done this, it is great.

I have never been a prude or a kill joy, I have enjoyed my life and have very few regrets and why not. You don't want other people to pay for your follies, you take that responsibility on yourself, pay for your own mistakes as a man should.

I have been thinking of what I would like to do with my two weeks in Oz and as I sit on this plane looking at the postcards that Caroline sent me, I know I will visit the court a few days and the rest of the time, weather permitting, I shall do some painting perhaps for this little book but will try to describe the colours described by Caroline on her cards particularly in a place called Byron Bay., as Caroline wrote 'Hope you like the card, I got one that looked nice for you to paint it shows all of Byron Bay too'.

I asked her to find me some nice places to paint, so this must be one of the places for me to go to paint, also the tree that the backpackers and the Mayor of Bundaberg planted in her memory, not all people are bastards and I have always had great confidence in our young people, after all it's their world now. I don't need to waste my time in a court room plus I don't think it would do me any good. I have confidence in the rule of the law, it does not need me for that. The evidence is important to prove guilt or innocence.

5th October

Arrived safe and well in Australia after a bumpy flight, I expect it is all in a day's work for the pilot and air crew. Richard was waiting for me in Bundaberg, great to see him. Our British consul was there to meet us in

Brisbane and to travel with us to Bundaberg, she helped get us through the airports with as little fuss as possible, this really helped after such a long flight. The help and support that we have received from Australia has been outstanding, as it was in UK. What more can one ask, and then to say a very big thank you. Just a few words to the awaiting media at Bundaberg airport and then away for a shower and a short rest. Lunch in Bundaberg TV. and press again and into court. The thing I have been most dreading, seeing the defendant in the flesh.

The court room was small and simple yet dignified, with the Supreme Court Judge who seemed very young to me but the court was handled with great dignity.

On looking at the defendant I felt not hatred, anger or the need for revenge but at that moment the man looked empty and pale, mere shale or a wax dummy of a man, it was almost unreal.

I had never been into a court before and hope I shall never have to attend one again in this way. Hopefully all will be over in a few days from now. I feel that things are now coming to an end, my dear son Richard has grown up very quickly in many ways. My daughter Caroline has touched the world with her simple love and the brave way she met her end. I am so sad of course but a very proud father. We always said we would have great children and that we surely did. Marjorie was a great mother to them and I always tried to be a loving caring father, what more can one do in life, you do your best at the time.

As I sit in this beautiful garden in Australia and listen to the birds, look at the colour of the early morning sky and I am taken back to when Caroline was here, I wonder when she awoke that last morning, what did she do, think or wonder about the day, she was so happy she was most likely thinking of her future, University, new friends and aims in life, so soon to be savagely ended along with our hopes and dreams too. These thoughts a few years ago were unthinkable, the tragic thing that has happened was certainly not in the equation.

6th October

Radio interview with John Lawes. No court today so spent the day at the Botanical gardens painting Caroline's memorial tree, the weather is warm and bright. We met one of the ladies we met last time we were there, Ann Duffy of the Rose Garden tea rooms, a bright energetic lass from Lancashire, full of humour and good fun, we had a good laugh, she could laugh for England, she deservedly won Toast Master of the year award, not surprisingly. We had a fine lunch courtesy of the same for Richard, Megan, Jan and myself.

Made a start on the painting of the tree, should be OK. Richard made a start too, should be good fun, Dad and young lad. The painting I hope to include in my book called the Bridge. I use the tree as a symbol of new life and new growth.

In the afternoon we all went to Childers, the scene of the dreadful tragedy, where fifteen young backpackers were burnt to death. The whole place has been rebuilt as a wonderful memorial and with thanks to Bill Trevor, who's inspiration was not lost even though he took the loss very personally, affecting him both physically and emotionally. He is a man who has inspired so many people to carry on and rebuild their lives. The memorial is most impressive, an art gallery with a painting of all the youngsters together, brilliantly executed and very emotional to see. The feelings are extraordinary, so much sadness and yet so much joy at the same time, very moving.

Megan Hunt from the British consulate has been outstanding and has been there every step of the way for us all, she has not only given her time, and expertise but she has shown warmth, caring and energy, that which, at times, we lack very much. A good day, busy but I am now very tired. It is all very draining but the highlight for today was meeting Bill Trevor, such an inspiration.

7th October

The day dawned warm and bright though a little windy I worked on the tree of life painting by the pool, very pleasant for eight am.

After breakfast we all went painting, I thought it a good idea to paint the Burnett bridge after a great deal of thought. The first part of the river looked beautiful as the water flashed it's highlights in the morning sun. It would be good to remember it that way further down the bridge is where the murder of Caroline occurred.

It looks such a beautiful place but these terrible crimes can happen anywhere in the world now.

The day went well, Richard and I painted by the river and Janet went to look at the shops in the town of Bundaberg, a very pleasant clean town, lot's of shops and expanses of building and development, good for the future to come.

Invited out to dinner by the Mayor of Bundaberg, Kay McDuff and city councillors. It was a good evening, good fellowship, it's no sin to laugh from time to time, Richard was in good form and is very well thought of by all, he is doing his best to make something good out of a disaster. I am very proud of him, it gives so much hope for the future in all ways, these types of things make you take care of what you have yet always keeping in your heart that which you have lost. "memories stay for ever", people, no!

Australia is a very beautiful country, wide open spaces and excellent climate, would I wish to live here? I am not sure. Number one country on my list is New Zealand but owning a second home in another country is not always easy, I am starting to look to my future which must be a good sign and a change of environment can only be helpful. I don't want to leave England completely but it would be nice to have everlasting summers.

8th October

A changeable day, windy-dull-bright and warm. All ready for court but unfortunately it has been postponed again, restarts Monday. This is frustrating but cannot be helped, it happens. So we made the best of the day, I had a swim in the pool then made some more headway with the Burnett bridge painting, my heart is not in it, nor is it for the tree of life, I am just going through the motions.

We went to Bundaberg for lunch for a break. Kath from our B&B drove us into town approx. eight miles each way. As there is nothing doing today at court we took the time to see around the area a little. We order a hire car for tomorrow, we are going to a small town called 1770 it is where Captain Cook landed in 1770 so we are looking forward to that.

9th October

The day dawned clear and bright, no wind. We collected the car and Richard drove Jan and I to the town 1770. Home from home having a Yorkshire connection.

It was so good to get away for the day, no one else around and into the beautiful countryside, so vast and different to anywhere else you could imagine, with it's small water holes, gum trees, cattle and, of course, Kangaroos.

To be by the sea, in the cool, was a joy, the colours magnificent. Richard and I did a painting which, for a change, we wanted to do, and enjoyed doing them.

I painted a large mango tree, I don't know how old it is, perhaps Captain Cook had his mangoes from it when he was searching for fresh water three hundred or more years ago.

We had lunch which in Oz can take some time, no problem, the food is very good and consists of locally caught fish and wonderful natural juices. No wonder Richard and Caroline like it here. We finished our paintings, Richard did two, we reluctantly started on our way back to Bunbaberg and to return the hire car. On our way back we call in at the Botanical Gardens to photograph Caroline's tree just in case we don't have the time to come back. There was a wedding taking place, they looked so happy as they passed us on a beautiful old steam train, and so life goes on. It was touch and go returning from 1770 when we encountered a snake in the middle of the road and had to swerve to avoid it, phew! Back at our B&B

satisfied with a day well spent, I, at least, went out like a proverbial light.

10th October
Sunday dawned, another beautiful day in Oz. I understand why people like it, especially the young. Sad news about one of the hostages in Iraq. Why do people do this? My heart goes out to the family, I do know how it feels.

We have been invited to afternoon tea with the Mayor and councillors after they have presented the keys of the city to Chantel, an eighteen year old paraolympic medal winner. Despite her disability, she achieved six medals for swimming, an amazing young lady. There was a great feeling of pride and a good family, it made us all feel good, just to be there, a real privilege.

That afternoon was when Bundaberg have their multi-cultural food festival, not only foods to taste but the enjoyment of a mix of cultural music, steel band, pan pipes and local children singing and playing instruments, a real happy atmosphere, if it could always be like this what a beautiful world we could have.

We sat with the Mayor Kay McDuff and the councillors and were introduced to Chantel and her Mom, lovely people. We had a splendid afternoon tea, a good chat and a laugh which makes you feel better. I also had a chance to thank the lady who gave me the butterfly design on my last sad visit. I am now finding this is a caring, growing, vibrant town.

The day passed well, lots going on in the cultural exhibition with lots of people. A good day. It is so important that we know life goes on and we get on with our daily lives. Being here makes me more sure that life goes on. Richard is doing an outstanding job and is very much admired by old and young alike. I have noticed he is very much like me, he wants to see something of this world while he is young. I think it's great, because Caroline was also of that mind. See the world, enjoy life, but not all are ordained to do so.

Note
In the court where I shall attend soon I have been made aware of a lady sitting in the public seats, I am informed she is a medium! and will insist on giving messages regarding what has gone on and is, of course, doing so, this is after befriending Richard, who neither needs or wants this intrusion. Mediumship, in it's right place, is all very well but in these circumstances can prove both distressing and annoying. On no account should this so called gift be used in this manner unless it is asked for.

11th October
Get ready for day in court. Witnesses, graphologist, Toxicologist, prison officers etc. all took the stand and either confirmed or denied the evidence

against the accused. What was to happen this day in court was extraordinary to say the least, it confirmed to me that human nature and the overall goodness of people, no matter what or who are or what they have done, is the overall feeling of doing what they feel is right. High sparks of truth and honour did I see in court this day and more so, because it put people's own safety and lives at risk! I am not going to write the names of the people involved but these deeds touched my heart and brought a feeling of joy, not only bringing things clearly to mind of what had happened on that fateful day 10th April 2002 but enabled me as a father, and Richard as a brother, to see some kind of result in the not too distant future, enabling us to draw a line under what has happened.

A very profound statement by one of the people giving evidence went as such "I wanted to do something right in my life, Caroline's family need to bring this matter to an end". A young person, who when he spoke these words from the witness box, looked directly at Richard and me, the tears began to well in his eyes, and mine, this was truly a brave man. I thank him for what he has done and hope the future years will treat him well.

This is not the only incident this day, that touched my heart, a young man gave me his condolences as I entered the court, so much feeling was let out this day. A young man, who had known the accused, also gave evidence, he was there with his family, he has two little boys and a good strong woman partner for support, he came to me in tears and shook my hand. These people are not saints, none of us are, but basically have honest hearts and wish to put right something that is in their hearts and minds. Others gave evidence this day who were brave in what they were saying, they did themselves great honour in doing so, asking nothing in return, this again gives me faith in human kind. It can be no more than simple love. Myself and what is left of my little family has been destroyed forever. Caroline's memory will always be in our hearts and we must go on alone on our long journey of life. This day has also confirmed to me that even people who live in the different ways to us have a code of honour and this type of crime is despised by them, a young girl's life for a few dollars and a mobile phone is abhorrent to them. Brave men and women, I salute you for what you have done and the risk you are taking. Truth will conquer all.

12th October
Once again the day dawned bright and sunny. Ready for another day in court with it's ups and downs, highs and lows, you don't know where all the bits and pieces fit. One of the most distressing things was all the details and photographs regarding Caroline's murder and videos of her covered body at the murder scene. I am quite sure it was of great importance to the case and every aspect has to be covered. To see such

a beautiful place in bright sunlight and the singing of the myriad of birds that once saw such an evil act take place such a short time before. Caroline's covered body looked small lying at the base of the bridge, all the area had been cordoned off, of course, a beautiful place, so sad and touched so many people around the world. The evil deed of night shall be brought into the light of day.

All the exhibits are listed in the court by the Supreme Judge who controls all the proceedings. This is done with great dignity and fairness, sometimes, even a little humour.

One of the exhibits were Caroline's shoes that had been thrown off her feet on impact. They looked so small, I am imagining her last terrified moments, tears are welling up in my eyes and my heart begins to bleed for what has been done. The fall from the Burnett bridge took under two seconds, it is my understanding that death was instant, I understand that the brain can live a further three minutes before it too dies, what happened in those few short moments, what did she think of? What was the last terrifying moments when she was fighting for her possessions, handbag and mobile phone. What was she conscious of at that point, moments from the end of her short life? We can only speculate. Surely a horrific and terrifying time for a child who was so dearly loved by all who knew her. I like to think the angels took her as she fell and that she will wake anew in the realm of the spirit. All of us are only seconds away from our own mortality so we must use our time the best we can.

The accused man just sits impassive to what is going on with the hint of a smile as the defence is picking faults in some of the evidence against him. I don't feel one thing or another about the man, I don't know him and to feel hate would only destroy myself but to want revenge is only human, all I want is to see justice done. And the correct man charged with the offence. I would not wish any parent to have to go through this everlasting torment that is ours for eternity. I will find the strength to go on as will my son, Richard, who has made us so proud and his mother Marjorie, hopefully they will carry on with Caroline's Rainbow Foundation.

And so the day went on and the trial goes on and today also we remember the Bali bombing, the killing and maiming of so many Australians, we should remember them, also these murdering barbarians that do these cowardly things to other human beings. They will get their just desserts one day and perhaps if it is in the name of God, surely he would not want this insult put upon his name. Any fool can take life only God can give it.

13th October
Awoken by the singing of birds, the songs are strange to me, not thrush or

blackbird but kookaburra and bell birds of so many colours, it's like an everlasting rainbow of colours dancing on the winds and streaming through our senses bringing an iridescent light perhaps upward to heaven, just giving us complete joy of life and spring perhaps in our lives too. Forward and onward.

This day was very upsetting in the court with people claiming that they had killed Caroline and then being utterly humiliated by the prosecution. The barrister for the crown, an exceedingly capable man who appears to work with great care in every little detail of this, even to him, horrific murder. Court proceedings are extremely methodical and it takes time to bring all the evidence together from the very complex picture built up by the Police Department in Bundaberg.

Court has a lunch break from one pm, and resumes at two thirty pm. We could not face lunch after leaving the court and facing the media in its ranks outside. I decided to say very little about how I felt as I find it too distressing after hearing all the horrific details all over again.

I walked on the Burnett bridge, now very beautiful in the Australian sunshine with its scented flowers and the singing birds, hardly a scene of such terror for my daughter in the last moments of her life to be thrown some thirty feet from the bridge.

We returned to court feeling a little better after having a walk in the air and feeling the sun on our faces, but I keep thinking of Caroline buried in York in a cold, sunless grave, never to breathe the sweet air or feel the sun again, sent to her death by an evil man in such a violence and helplessness, it beggars belief.

The prosecution gave details of the trial and witnesses evidence over the past three weeks, painting a clear picture to all that had happened. Richard and I sat together with Janet holding hands for comfort. I could feel my heart breaking and life draining away as we were told of the last moments of Caroline's life, the telephone call to her friend Sarah and her last walk across the Burnett bridge that evening 10th April 2002.

There were many details, photographs of Caroline's body after what had happened. I was not present at the showing of these to the court but Richard has seen them all, this was something a young man should never be subjected to. The basic facts are that the assailant snatched her phone and then tried to take her bag, Caroline put up a struggle to stop him. He apparently kicked her to the ground, knocking out some of her teeth hitting her about the head and then swinging her around in this brutal attack. When she was screaming, bloodied, her little face broken and in a defenceless state, he picked her up and threw her off the Burnett bridge. She screamed in terror, her screams were heard by many people as she fell into the darkness to her death. Beneath the bridge people have made a little shrine and bring flowers and toys to remember her gentle little spirit. This is all I can write, this is the truth of what happened in the year of our Lord, two thousand and two on the 10th April in Bundaberg, Queensland, Australia.

This picture paints it's story and has broken many people's hearts, many have shed tears, many blame themselves for not being there in some way, no one is to blame but the murderer who perpetrated this dastardly crime against a young woman with so much to offer in her future years. Richard and I talked to the press, Richard told them what he was doing with the Rainbow Foundation he and his mother had set up in Caroline's name, the rainbow I had depicted in my last painting I did with my little helper, now it seems so long ago in time and space.

So time passes and we are returned to our B&B where we are staying, before doing so we return to the Botanical gardens to see once again the memorial tree, it is to me indeed the tree of life for all of us who are in this breathing and hectic world and those who have passed into the world beyond are aware of it too.

14th October

Went into court, taken by the police, they have been very supportive in all this matter through the past years. The Crown Prosecution had spoken yesterday with their opinion of what had happened on that fateful night showing points and counter points of the available proof of what done, of course, with great confidence in such a high profile case and such a capable silk.

Court opened and the defence lawyer gave his case again with great command of the English language, a very capable and eloquent man giving different interpretations of the evidence he had before him, times, dates, places etc. which we can all see from a different angle and perspective. It is important to look at all the evidence you have, I am so glad we have such a system of law in our respective countries.

After lunch the High Court Judge gave his summing up to the jury, giving them all the evidence he has to hand and giving all the points of law. Emphasis was on proof brought forward. In my opinion, the judge was very profound, covering all aspects and appeared completely unbiased, leading not one way or the other.

Court was adjourned until tomorrow when hopefully a verdict will be reached. All I ask now is for justice to be done. I would not like to see the wrong man convicted, we are all innocent until proven guilty, this is how it should be.

Has this really happened or has it all been a nightmare, is this all in my mind? I have proof it is all real, I saw her body battered and bruised and said goodbye to her in England, burying her in the Yorkshire clay, no one can ever hurt her again and her heart will always be breathing in mine.

She was conceived in Greece with love, lived with a loving family in Yorkshire and died screaming in Australia. Will the end of this story ever be!!

15th October
Early to court when all there was left to do was to instruct the jury once again of their duty and send them out to deliberate. We can do nothing but wait, and that is what we did after a few interviews.

The police, as good as ever, took us to the Botanical Gardens once more where we had coffee and painted all day. We had a surprise visit from Kay McDuff, the Mayor, and saw our now dear friend Ann at the tea rooms, making us welcome as usual with tea and her famous Eccles cakes, all helped to pass this long day.

The weather was warm with a gentle breeze, the work went quite well with stops for tea and a visit to the new Japanese gardens.

A phone call from the police that the jury were back and now one mad dash to get back to the court house, we can't miss the verdict after this long wait. We arrive in time after running across a road and flying up the steps, just in time, I have a feeling they were waiting for us. The jury were on their feet, I was there, fingers crossed, their names were read out, and so the scene was set. Silence fell, so intense it was that it was as though even the birds stopped sing. They were asked for the first verdict **Guilty** of robbery, there was a stunned silence, the second verdict **Guilty of murder**. Stunned silence turned to a lively excitement, the whole court seemed to breathe a sigh of relief. The correct result, justice had been done. It had been conducted with great dignity in all ways, also a great coverage, another milestone has passed. Truth had been proven without doubt. The guilty man just shrugged as if to say 'well it's what I expected'. There were other charges taken into account, these were duly dealt with.

The court fell silent once again as the judge passed sentence, ten years for robbery with violence and life imprisonment for murder for such a despicable crime in ending a young life in a violent and cruel way, I can say no more, justice has been done and will now take it's place in history.

My daughter, Caroline Ann Stuttle, will now always be part of this beautiful part of Australia and hope she will always be remembered with love and joy, inspiring other like minded young people to spread their wings throughout our beautiful world.

Court closed and we went out into a quiet room for a few moments of reflection. I walked out to meet the world media waiting on the steps in an eerie silence for a change. I simply thanked them for the privacy that they had afforded Richard and myself during our stay here, also thanking

Police, both in Australia and England, for their continued support and the British consulate officials who had, in their special way, made an easier passage for us 'Thank you, Megan', I have to mention the people of Bundaberg who have been most kind, but to Kay McDuff, the Mayor, an extra special and loving thank you for the time shared with us in her busy schedule.

This horrific crime has touched the hearts of many and will continue to do so. And so the day ended. We go for a small celebration of which I shall not write, but it was good, such a relief. As for my son Richard and myself, it is as though a huge weight has been lifted from us, we can now walk into the future and pick up the things that we would like to do with what is left of our lives, with an enhanced need to enjoy the time we have. Let us take an example from Caroline, bubbling with enthusiasm at the prospect of exploring new countries, making new friends and, especially, her years at University, this must not go to waste. Perhaps it is not the length of life but how we use our time, Caroline used it well, let her life be an example to others, let that be her legacy.

We must now start to say goodbye to Caroline and let her go on her journey over the rainbow bridge there to follow her dreams as we should all follow ours and perhaps we will met again on that far away shore.

16th October
Say goodbye to Bundaberg today; start for Brisbane. Richard and I did a small interview for a Brisbane newspaper with photographs. I think we've had enough, interviews - up to the neck in them. Looking forward to the end of this circus now. Had a walk in Bagara, a beautiful place, warm and pleasant, even had a paddle in the sea, a house here would be pleasant who knows, maybe New Zealand. Start thinking of the future,

perhaps a move would be good for all concerned. Had lunch here with a Bundy, ginger beer, very nice. Back to the B&B and then to the airport, driven, very kindly, by Kath who has looked after us so well during our stay. Kay McDuff came to see us off at the airport, that was a nice surprise and, thank goodness, no cameras or press. Off on our forty five minute flight to Brisbane, a pleasant flight, if not a little bumpy, and so goodbye to Bundaberg with a little sadness, they are such nice people.

Brisbane - a very clean city, so good, no TV. cameras or interviews here. Friends text from England on how the news of the result had been received, apparently I came over with dignity and respect, unlike, and these are not my words 'the glamed up beached whale who wants all to feel sorry for her' (some don't) but that's enough of that, it is not a popularity show or a show of any kind and all should be now left to melt away...

A nice relaxing evening in Brisbane, don't feel like eating much, expect this is the end of something and the start of something new. Had a restless nights sleep in the hotel, The Royal on the Park, it had been so nice and quiet in Bagara, the noise is so disturbing, tyres squealing and engines revving.

17th October

Up early and we are greeted by the sound of fire engines, yes, the hotel may be on fire, could it happen to anyone else! All ok. and under control, did not have to evacuate, also it started to rain which is good for the land and certainly badly needed, we seem to bring it wherever we go - 'rain dancer'.

Richard came to the hotel and we went to collect the hire car, all done and dusted in fifteen minutes, very impressive. The write up in the Brisbane Sunday Mail was very well written, hopefully this the last we shall see on this matter, I sincerely hope so, perhaps we can now chart the end of the media mayhem.

We drove to Byron Bay and stopped on the way at Surfers Paradise, really beautiful sand, white and fine with surf coming into the eighty kilometre long beach, the young people enjoy this, even I do. We continue on to Byron Bay, it starts to get dull and grey, not unlike Scotland or the common at Strensell but the land is dry, now we have brought the rain here too, perhaps from the UK. maybe next week, when we return, we shall have snow in Scarborough! We arrive in Byron and it started to rain and rain, tears from the sky. It is fortunate that we have a car to allow us to have a drive around and get the area formulated in our minds. Perhaps we have tears from heaven, Caroline spent four weeks here and it was so impressed on her mind, she must have been so happy the last few weeks and days of her life so I hope the sun will smile on me in the week that I am here then I can paint something of this beautiful area and start saying goodbye and thank you for your dreams, I hope they were happy for they will have to last forever. We went into the little town for dinner, that was pleasant but rather cold as the rain was coming down in buckets. Perhaps tomorrow the sun will shine on me as it did on her such a short time ago in 2002. All I have now are the postcards, these I can touch and read, so on it goes and I would like to do some painting, and so would Richard.

18th October
Slept well at Byron Bay, the poet's settlement in Australia. The sky is still grey with lots of rain and windy but it has got time to clear up, hopefully this weather will improve and I can attempt the two paintings I would like to take home with me. One, of course, is the lighthouse and one going the opposite way across the beautiful beach, what I have seen to date, I have liked. This place is very popular with the young people, life outdoors with the beach and the countryside they form quite a community amongst themselves. Caroline was backpacking and it must have been like a bit of paradise, especially when the sun was out.

Rain continued throughout the day and showed no sign of stopping but we made the best of things (sunshine every day would be boring) we drove to a beautiful place called the Crystal Castle where there were the most beautiful gardens with a laid out labyrinth which Richard and his friend Matthew explored in the rain. There were crystals set in rocks as we walked to the entrance. In one room there was an amazing art gallery of very ethereal paintings, quite outstanding. The other rooms contained all manner of crystals with explanations to go with them and very helpful knowledgeable staff, the book shop held a wide selection on all sorts of things spiritual, healing as well as crystal. Every subject was displayed very well, there was a healing centre and an opportunity for spiritual readings also, fascinating. An excellent place to visit indeed but the weather was not kind to us at all.

Byron Bay town is full of interesting shops of all type of goods, multi colour displays of wondrous objects. The didgeridoo's were spectacular to say the least, all shapes and sizes. Richard has really developed his ability to play his but fortunately he is not playing in confined places.

Richard is, of course, a fine chef and we decided, as the weather was so bad, it was not a good idea to go out again to eat. Dinner was very good indeed; local fish, salmon, swordfish and tuna; great selection and so nice to see a master chef at work.

The day spent, the rain coming down in torrents and the wind blowing a gale. We all called it a day, perhaps tomorrow will bring a little reprieve, I doubt it, it looks set for some time yet. Perhaps it's a lesson in life, you don't always get what you expect but what you need. It would be good to have sun and gentle sea and a glass of wine, but the land desperately needed the rain, perhaps more than we needed the sun. In a few days all this will be history and we must do what we can in the time we have. Rain, hail or shine life goes on, thanks be to God.

Janet had a tarot reading today which was very positive for all and informative, perhaps about future times and events, it gave a little boost to things, it's good to do this sometimes if only for fun, the good things will come. We can link it with the saying 'why chase the butterflies, when if you stand still the butterflies will land on you'. Stand back and be still, a good idea for most things (especially now).

19th October

So it goes on, the wind, rain and thunder and then a surprise, it has stopped raining and we manage to make a start on the paintings of Byron. As soon as the sun came out so did the people in droves. I don't know how they get such suntans, nice to see them all happy. A good day and a good start to the painting, I would like to do two if possible. Feeling much lighter now and the weight has been lifted from my shoulders, yes, there is an end, and light at the end of a long, long road.

At this stage it is very important to stay positive in what you want to do with the rest of your life because hopefully there is still more to come, perhaps it is also important to be happy once more in your personal life, though much of the bitterness will never heal, it is best left buried where it should always stay.

Richard made dinner, nice to have such a talented son. We spent the evening talking and laughing. Richard's friend, Matthew, is staying with us which is good for Richard to have one of his mates for company. Janet has purchased some new healing cards and gave us all a fun reading, all very positive.

Me! Well I need to say goodbye in my own way, just a couple of paintings to make and there we should leave all this to go into the realms of history, nothing can change things now, we must accept all that has happened in this past extraordinary time of change for all of us. So fingers crossed for a reasonable day. I hope for less wind and NO RAIN.

20th October

Beautiful morning, no wind or rain even some sunshine. I feel nice and relaxed and rested a lot better. Janet and I went to the beach and saw crabs, beautiful shells, white sand, peace and quiet, except for the birds, the blue green sea of the pacific ocean where dolphins and whales pass so near to the shoreline. Beautiful, fresh and clean, what more could you have. With this weather holding perhaps I can get some paintings worked on today.

Great, worked on two paintings, they went ok. Just to finish off this journey of discovering many parts of myself that I had never known or forgotten during the past thirty or more years of looking after wife and children, where has the time gone? Where do I go from here? Perhaps it is in the lap of the Gods where I go, what we do in life and how and when we meet our end. The three stages in life, to be born, to have life, however long or short and to die, of this we can be sure.

I like Byron Bay and can see why Caroline liked it so much, the beautiful colours, wonderful sea, blue sky, good fresh food and cost of living not too expensive. Surfing and lots of shops with so many items to delight the young people. A little bit of paradise for the retail therapy shopper.

I made the journey to the Byron lighthouse standing at the most easterly point in Australia, the vast expanse of sea where whales and dolphins are a common sight, this was a small journey but a meaningful one. Many will make this journey but to me stepping along that same pathway, it was very meaningful and a letting go at the same time, with the numerous bird calls that I do not know, the swallows streaking across the sky which is now turning different colours as we look across the distant hills to where our journey in life may lead us on the wings of time, leading us ever to new experiences which is the purpose of life, to feel, to cry, to laugh but most of all, to love.

I watched an Australian TV. programme with great interest, a man was giving away his home to help fund the protection of the environment. Giving his life's work away, in fact, he said he didn't need it anymore and wanted to protect the earth. Very commendable. Perhaps the rich cannot pass through the eye of a needle for we can not take possessions with us only our deeds. How very profound in thought, what do any of us need? We spend our life getting, not seeing what we should be seeing and doing this is a very simple truth which we can learn so much. You don't need to give your house away but we could all manage with less.

And so the day went by in a very pleasant way. Richard and I did some painting, Janet some shopping, and Matthew some walking and writing. Richard made a wonderful dinner, then a relaxing evening was had by all.

21st October

The last full day for us dawned bright but windy, so as disasters like floods, thunderstorms and torrential rain has been all around us we decide to make one last effort and finish our two watercolours. We kept at it until one pm. When it started to rain, we packed up and went back to our apartment for lunch, then the sun came out so we all walked down to the local beach called Tallows Beach. We had a really long leisurely walk, the best we have had. I am feeling a lot more relaxed in myself. I know this is the letting go of past times and looking to the future, that I know will change so now, as I have done for many years, live for the day as tomorrow never comes.

As we walk by the sea, the waves racing up to wet our feet, it was a little like walking in paradise, walking on the soft white sand, our footprints showing a clear step forward into the distant future or past as the sea washed away our prints as if we had never been. A clear new start to a clear new time. We can never go back but as the sand and sea have taught us we have a new start every day, washed clean again. We must not lose sight of our hopes and dreams. A beautiful time, a little bit of heaven enjoyed by all.

This the final evening in Byron Bay. Out at sea we observe lightening and a little thunder, it was truly awesome in the real sense of the word. The flashes of the lightening silhouetting the clouds miles out to sea deep and full of dark mysteries we know not of. The stars were bright and the moon seemed to shine with all the brightness of heaven and the blue velvet night enfolded the earth. Caroline must have seen this during her stay here, she also walked on the sand, swam in the sea, laughed and enjoyed the company of friends and now the sea has washed away her footprints forever. Where is she, I thought this night, perhaps a twinkling little star shining amongst the myriad of stars, as my mother told me when I was a child, the stars are the windows to heaven. So my last evening was spent thinking of what had been, looking at the vast heavens and walking on the ever changing sand of which we are all part of for eternity, perhaps a billion galaxies of times future.

Today Richard collected a butterfly. He put it on his t-shirt to dry out as it's wings were wet from all the rain. It stayed on Richard as we all walked around, back at the garden by our apartment he placed it on a leaf, next time we looked it had flown away.

22nd October

Departed from Byron Bay in beautiful sunshine, had one hour, the sky was so blue it made the sea sparkle in the morning sun. What a shame to leave such a beautiful place, but now back to Brisbane. Well, I have seen this place in all it's moods and shades. Looking back, this was a good thing I should.

Our drive to Brisbane was very pleasant, Richard drives very well, we arrive back at our hotel, again The Royal on the Park. It is very good, we were looked after well. We have lunch in the town and then went to the British Consulate office where we met up with Megan Hunt, the Vice Consul, who has looked after us so well and to meet the new Consulate General who has taken an interest in the case regarding Caroline etc. We spent a pleasant hour there and it was nice to see one of my paintings in the office (The Heart of York). It seems so long ago that it was painted now.

Weather now very pleasant and warm, we had two hours of daylight left before going out for a wonderful dinner, what a lovely way to say goodbye to Brisbane, for the time being anyway. There are so many English people here, perhaps I should start a studio here! Who knows! Very tempting but it is so very far away from my beloved Yorkshire. Climate is good, colours are wonderful, the food is so fresh and plentiful and there is plenty of space. At the end of our evening we walk back to our hotel. Brisbane is just as noisy as York or Scarborough, with some drunken halfwits shouting "f*** you guy's" in a different accent. Perhaps this is a thing of the future, why can't they leave people alone. Drink and drugs are now always going to be part of this world culture, it is something we could do without because the yobs can't handle it, so please go and look at yourselves first, thank you.

Thus ended a pleasant night in Brisbane, very tired and very warm. I felt more decisive about what I wanted to do, which was for the first time more positive, I certainly do not want now what I had - I must move forward.

23rd October

Departure day from Brisbane and from Australia. Very warm and very sunny and beautiful colours. Have a little walk into the town then into the Botanical Gardens to paint the river and the bridge with Richard. It is so hot and very quiet. There are the most beautiful Jacaranda trees in full blossom, also a dragon tree one of the two in Australia. Apparently Stradivarius used the oil for his violins (dragon oil). I remember seeing his house in Cremona, Italy, where I visited and worked not so long ago. And so the day went on, we finished painting, went into the town for lunch, and spent a little time browsing in the Brisbane Art Gallery where there were large very impressive digital photographs, I would like to have seen some local paintings but did not have enough time.

Richard took us to the airport, no problem and we said goodbye, I never like long farewells at airports - too emotional, just a hug and see you in New Zealand next year and on our way.

The check in, of course, has long queues. As we waited we were taken out of line and ferried to an empty check in and very kindly taken to the VIP lounge, what a treat, where we could have a shower and freshen up, have a little snack in comfort and relax until our flight was called. I get a little embarrassed at all the attention but due to the situation people have bent over backwards to make life easier for us. It is with thanks to these companies that have helped to make the passage more comfortable, so many thanks to Emirates, Quantas, and, of course, once again to our British Consulate.

We are now ready for our long flight back to Birmingham and onward to Scarborough where the cold and wet awaits us, a little different from the hot sun we have experienced these last few days. England does have plenty of water which Australia is so desperate for at the moment.

I am at present sitting in a first class seat upgraded by Emirates airline, an airline which I have flown with many times but in economy class. What a change it is to have plenty of space, we are so lucky. We were upgraded from Brisbane to Singapore to business class but were not guaranteed any further upgrade after that, so this is just amazing, so kind and thoughtful, it once again shows to me how much Caroline has touched people's hearts. I do feel a bit of a fraud sitting here with all this luxury when little daughter had to save so hard for her economy ticket and I have been given it because of her.

It's very bumpy so it's hold tight and fingers crossed, it will be so good to step on the ground again, don't we all feel like that sometimes in many ways.

And so we pass through the night, looking at stars through the window of this beautiful powerful aircraft as it speeds me back to my beloved England where my memories and dreams once were and this journey has given us all a chance to dream again for the ever hopeful future years. It has always been in God's hands and that is the truth. As my grandmother used to say all those years ago 'tell the truth and shame the devil' doing right for us at the time but it may not be so in a years time who knows, life is full and so strange.

Will the memory of Caroline's brutal murder help make young people more aware in future times, I do hope so, the trouble is, we all forget. Being young and feeling indestructible will always come with it's risks as does what we do and where we go, being young and free should be the best time of your life, that is why I have always maintained - let the children fly, let them follow their dreams but, as a parent, instil in them the importance of the safety aspect. How many do, no matter how many times they are told to be cautious and think things out carefully. Let's hope things get better for our young people, I do hope so but we have to remember that the drug culture is very much with us now just under the surface waiting to ruin young peoples lives and their families as it has mine. So we should all be very much aware of this at all times. Things are not as they seem, and as parents, we would wish.

As I write the words on my return to UK. and the ending of countless words and feelings that have passed through my mind, I must bring these thoughts and feelings to an end, though it will never end for a bereaved parent or a grieving son, for a murdered sister, it will always be with us as part of us also has been savagely taken from us, we must go on and learn to let go, our loved one has travelled over that rainbow bridge, let us use those colours to move forward with our lives until we too cross that same bridge. The body may turn to dust and decay but the spirit lives for eternity.

The bursary I have set up as the 'Richard and Caroline Painting Fund' at Huntington school will now go on as long as Richard and I live and hopefully will inspire young people of the future to paint, draw or make music and they in their time can pass on the knowledge to our children's children. What more can anyone expect, we can never demand of anyone, what would anyone like to be remembered for, who knows what will be said of us. I think I would like to be remembered, not as an artist who has painted York and Yorkshire people, who has worked in Italy, Switzerland, Australia, New Zealand etc. I would like to be remembered as someone who fulfilled a part of a dream that I had so long ago, a wife, son and daughter.

I would like to be remembered as someone who, when told you can not make a living doing a job that you love, would do it with all my strength and make a success of it. Most of all, I would like to be remembered as a one man who was not afraid to make mistakes, for half a dream fulfilled leaves dreams of the future to unfold. We may want the moon but look forward to the stars.

Use your talents to make this world a better, safer, more beautiful place always, God be in your dreams and enjoy and use the many talents that you have been so freely given.

Use your time well, do not let time use you.......